Old Kanawha Baptist Church Minutes —Indexed—

Plus Unpublished County Court Records of West Virginia

Eugene Lincoln Peck
and
Regina Peck Andrus

HERITAGE BOOKS
2014

HERITAGE BOOKS

AN IMPRINT OF HERITAGE BOOKS, INC.

Books, CDs, and more—Worldwide

For our listing of thousands of titles see our website
at
www.HeritageBooks.com

Published 2014 by
HERITAGE BOOKS, INC.
Publishing Division
5810 Ruatan Street
Berwyn Heights, Md. 20740

International Standard Book Numbers
Paperbound: 978-0-7884-0735-2
Clothbound: 978-0-7884-6004-3

Dedication

This booklet was done as a meager way to say "Thank you" to all the people who have contributed to the volumes of genealogical material in libraries across the country that we have gratefully tapped into. Hopefully, others will find this small booklet useful in their own searches.

TABLE OF CONTENTS

Page blank in original

Page blank in original

Page blank in original

Acknowledgments

Without the persistent efforts of Ellen Calvert in tracking down the whereabouts of the Old Kanawha Baptist Church Minutes, we would not be able to provide a transcription of the minutes for interested readers. We are grateful to her for providing us with a Xerox copy of the minutes to use for transcription, and for all her help in our own personal research. We also would like to thank her for providing us with her personal accounts of the events related to finding the missing Mason County, West Virginia records at the University of West Virginia at Morgantown.

We would never have contacted Mrs. Calvert had her name not been given to us by our distant relative Hazel Peck, of Leon, West Virginia. Hazel was our first "living" contact in Mason County, West Virginia. She welcomed us with opened arms and has provided us with useful information and many other fruitful contacts over the years.

We would also like to thank the patient and helpful librarians at the West Virginia and Regional History Collection in Colson Hall at the University of West Virginia at Morgantown for supplying us with the information on, and the status of, the microfilming project currently under way. They have also been of great help in our personal research.

Our families have been wonderful for putting up with our "boring" genealogical talk, and for their support during all our time devoted to research, transcription and the writing process, during this and other projects. You are greatly appreciated.

THE OLD KANAWHA BAPTIST

CHURCH MINUTES

THE OLD KANAWHA BAPTIST CHURCH MINUTES

Introduction

    The minutes of the Kanawha Baptist Church of Pratt, Kanawha County, West Virginia (dating from July 1796 through August 1845), are transcribed in a manner that seeks to retain the original spelling, mistakes, capitalization, punctuation and general look of the document. These minutes do not appear to be the originals written by John Hansford, the early Clerk of the Kanawha Church; instead they appear to be a handwritten copy made by an unidentified "JMJ" at a much later date. "JMJ" at times copied the same page twice, noted missing pages, and included late death dates (i.e., 1889, 1908) for some of the members.

    The actual manuscript used in transcribing the minutes is a Xerox copy obtained from Ellen Calvert, of Cabin Creek, West Virginia. The story of how Ellen Calvert obtained these minutes is related below:

Kanawha Baptist Church Minutes
by Ellen Calvert, 1984

The first permanent settlement in Kanawha County, WV, was made at Cedar Grove, about 16 miles south east of Charleston, by William Morris, his ten grown children, and their families. They had come from Culpeper Co., Virginia, by way of Monroe County, WV. They were Baptists, and had meetings in their fort, especially when John Alderson, well-known Shenandoah Valley minister and father-in-law of William Morris, Jr., visited.

Several years after 1773, when the settlement was made, one of William Sr's daughters and her husband, John Jones, moved across the Kanawha River from the settlement and established their home. Here, where Pratt, West Virginia is now located, Elder James Johnston organized the first Baptist Church in the Kanawha Valley. This was on 6 July 1796 and was called The Old Kanawha Baptist Church. A great many early settlers and westward bound migrants left their names on the old church records.

About 1940 I visited the church seeking information on my ancestor, one of William Morris's sons. The minister told me that no one living remembered a time when the minutes had been in the church. Existing minutes began about 1895, and no one knew what had become of minutes prior to that time.

A committee is now completing plans to have the town of Pratt declared an historic district in order to obtain federal funds for the restoration of existing old structures. The week before Christmas a member of this committee telephoned me to ask if I had any old dated documents that could be used to prove the age of Pratt. She knew of my great interest in the town. Later the same evening that she had called I was working on one of my genealogical problems and telephoned a friend in Charleston to ask his advice on my problem. During our conversation he asked where my early family settled and I told him Pratt. He replied, "Then you would be interested in reading my minutes of The Old Kanawha Baptist Church." I couldn't believe what I had just heard. He assured me that he had a copy of the original minutes. I didn't really believe it until I went to his home the next morning to see for myself. He very graciously allowed me to make photo copies for the Old Kanawha Baptist Church and myself. There were 145 pages covering the period of 1796 through 1850, leaving about 50 years of minutes still missing.

The first sentence of the minutes states that the church was organized in 1796; the information needed by the committee to prove the age of the Town of Pratt. A miracle for Christmas!

Using the Xerox copy as the basis for measurement, it appears that these minutes were written in a notebook that measured about 8 inches wide by 9 1/2 inches tall. The pages were mechanically numbered at some point, starting with number 21 and ending with number 132. The contents of the first twenty pages of the notebook are unknown, since those pages are not included in the Xerox copy.

The handwriting of the scribe is difficult to read at times. He was not precise nor consistent in forming his individual letters. It was easier to decipher his handwriting in the context of a sentence, but it was often hard to decipher individual names. His capital letters L and S appear to be identical most of the time, making it generally impossible to tell if a name is Lee or See. Lee was the name of one of the founders and pastors of the early Church, but I can not be certain that there was not also a family in the minutes by the name of See. The majority of the time the name looked like See, at times it could have been either, and only once in a while it appeared to obviously be Lee. Every time the name See appears, it could probably also be read as Lee. Other letters besides L and S also are difficult to distinguish from one another on occasion: u and n; a, u and d; y and g; and i, e, u, n, m, when all strung together.

Surnames are transcribed as they appear to be written, allowing the reader to make interpretations. At times I have included alternate renderings in brackets; for example, Manser [*Mauser*]. Such brackets are also used to indicate missing or unreadable portions of words, and brackets enclose explanatory information.

The scribe would occasionally use abbreviations, without leaving us a key to his meaning. Some of these abbreviations are easy to determine, others are not clear--the meanings remain open to interpretation. The scribe often uses standard abbreviations for months and Mister and Misses. A list of other abbreviations is below.

Abbreviations:	Meaning:
Adj, Ajd, AJ, etc.	Adjourned
Assn	Association
B	Baptism
B	Business
B, Br, B^r, Bro	Brother/s
B$\underline{ren}$	Brethren
C	Communion
C (above column of numbers)	Unknown
Ch	Church
Clk	Clerk
Dec^r	December
E (preceding a name)	Elder
E, E_	Experience
Feby, Feb^r	February
Geo	George
Jany	January
JH	John Hansford
JMJ	Unknown scribe
Mch	March
Nover, Nov^r	November
Ock	O'clock
Pr	Preaching
Pr	Property
pr	per
R$\underline{d}$, Rd, R^d, Recd, Rcd, Rec^d	Received
S~	Sister
S^d	Said
Sr, S$\underline{r}$, S^r	Senior
Wm, W^m, W$\underline{m}$	William

History of the Baptist Church

The Baptists were few in number before the Revolutionary War, but individual Baptists began to push across the Alleghenies into the northwestern part of Virginia in the 1770s. The Baptists had no organized churches at this time in the Virginia frontier county of Greenbrier (which covered most of present day West Virginia, excluding the present northern and eastern counties). When John Alderson, Jr. (1738-1821), the pastor of Linville Creek's Church in Rockingham County, Virginia, visited the area around 1775, he found "a wild, uncultivated place, in which Christ and His cross were seldom, if ever, preached, his bowels yearned toward the people. He proclaimed among them the pure Gospel." (History of the Baptists in Virginia, page 425, by Robert Baylor Semple.)

After his initial visit, Alderson returned to his home in Rockingham County. He was asked to come again to Greenbrier, baptizing one person on that trip, and two more on a subsequent trip, with two Baptists moving into the area. In 1777, he also moved to Greenbrier, just before the outbreak of Indian wars in the area. Safety concerns required the inhabitants to stay shut up in forts and blockhouses. He went from fort to fort with his ministry without seeing another Baptist preacher for seven years, often meeting resistance, but never ceasing his efforts. He established a small group in Greenbrier, which he considered to be an arm (or extension) of the Linville Creek church. Under his guidance, the Greenbrier Church was formed by twelve individuals in 1781, and became part of the Ketocton Association of Baptists. One reason for applying to the Association was the hope that more preachers might be sent into the area, although this did not occur. In 1793, all the churches west of the Blue Ridge mountains, including Greenbrier, were formed into the New River Association.

The first Baptist preacher to visit the area after John Alderson was James Johnston. He aided Elder Alderson in the establishment of the Indian Creek church in 1792, an arm of Greenbrier, and placed the church under the care of Mark Richards. Johnston also finally moved to the area, and by 1796 there were enough members in Kanawha Valley to warrant the establishment of another new church from the parent organization in Greenbrier. With the help of Elder Alderson, Elder James Johnston and twelve members organized the Kanawha Baptist Church on 6 July 1796.

Elder John Alderson remained the pastor of the Greenbrier church, but he also preached at the Kanawha Church, as can be seen in the minutes. From the Greenbrier church, Elder Alderson helped to establish seven other churches by 1810: Big Levels (1796), Teay's Valley (1805), Mud River (1807), Kanawha (1796), Cole River (1807), Indian Creek (1792), and Blue Stone (1804). Although Peter's Creek (1803) was not officially established by Alderson, it started as an arm of Kanawha, which he did establish. His name last appears in the Kanawha church minutes on 18 June 1809. He lived to be 83 and was buried in 1821 in the graveyard next to the Greenbrier church--the fourth Baptist church established within West Virginia boundaries.

The Kanawha church flourished greatly while under Elder Johnston. Elder Johnston's name appears in the Kanawha minutes a final time on February 1803. Sometime after that date he moved to Kentucky, leaving the congregation without a resident pastor. Below is a list of Baptist Elders mentioned, by dates recorded in the minutes:

Elders listed in the minutes:

Elder James Johnston	16 July 1796 -- 19 Feb 1803
Elder John Alderson	27 May 1797 -- 18 June 1809
Elder John Lee	20 May 1809 -- 20 June 1818
Elder John Morris	18 Apr 1818 -- 25 Sept 1824
Elder John Young	18 Sept 1819
Elder James Ellison	29 Nov 1823
Elder W^m.A. Wood	May 1825 -- June 1831
Elder W^m.C. Ligon	Nov 1832 -- Sept 1841
Elder Bradley	Sept 1839
Elder Mitchell	May 1842
Elder Wythel Wood	6 Oct 1843
Elder Maloy Rock	31 Dec 1843 -- July 1845

In 1801 the Greenbrier Association was formed from the New River Association. John Alderson was generally the moderator of the Association, with Josiah Osburne serving as the first clerk. Osburne was succeeded by Francis Crutchfield, who was considered by some to be one of the most accomplished scholars of that day, and a great educator.

The Association, consisting of four churches in 1801 (Greenbrier, Indian Creek, Big Levels or Lewisburg, and Kanawha), usually met annually the Friday before the second Sunday in September, and continued for three days. They received letters and delegates, gave advice and sent a circular letter from each meeting, and attended to requests of the churches--like the request for arbitration between Mikel Yates and John Jones, made by the Kanawha church to the twenty-one ministers and messengers attending an Association meeting held at John Hansford's meeting house on 21 Aug 1816. The case was not resolved by the local members, so a committee was formed, and a decision declared on the issue.

The Greenbrier Association 1803 meeting was hosted by the Kanawha church, the sessions being held in the Morris meeting house (a log house) on the northern side of the Kanawha River at Cedar Grove. The Association had gained one more church at Peter's Creek, and counted 287 members in 1803, 45 of which were in Kanawha.

By 1810 four more churches had been added to the Greenbrier Association--Teay's Valley, Mud River, Cole River and Blue Stone--with 277 members reported in all the churches except for Greenbrier and Blue Stone (the membership numbers for those two churches were not reported). The Kanawha membership had dropped to 33. [See Table 1].

Kanawha was part of the Greenbrier Association for fifteen years until the Teay's Valley Association was formed in 1812. In 1872, the Raleigh Association was formed from the Greenbrier Association, and Kanawha (called Paint Creek in the minutes) left Teay's Valley and joined with Raleigh, although it did not stay long. The Kanawha Valley Association was created by twenty-four churches located in Boone, Lincoln and Kanawha counties in April 1873. Because the Kanawha church was within the new Associations borders, it became one of the charter member churches.

The Kanawha church did not have a meeting house strictly its own for the first one hundred years. From 1798 to 1834 the meetings were held at member's homes or places listed:

John Morris, Peter's Creek, Morris Meeting House, John Hansford, Catherine Morris, John Jones, Nelson Priddy, Benjamin Morris, Levi Morris, Samuel Shrewsbury, Felix G. Hansford, Capt. John Harvey, Hansford Meeting House and Charles Venable.

From 1834 to 1857, the church met in a privately owned house, built specially for Baptist use by John Hansford, Sr. and his sons. This building was occupied and burned by Federal Soldiers during the Civil War.

After the war the meetings alternated between two Union church buildings at Hansford and Clifton (Clifton is an early name for Pratt), but the Kanawha church as a separate congregation seemed to be fading away without a place of their own. Money was collected and a new building started in 1890 in Pratt, Kanawha County, West Virginia, only to be lost to fire before completion. Another building was started on a new site, and this building was dedicated, free of debt, on the fifth Sunday in October 1892.

Over time the church membership outgrew this original building, and a new brick church was built near the site of the old one, with completion in 1968.

TABLE I -- BAPTIST GREENBRIER ASSOCIATION ABOUT 1810

Names of Churches	Constitution date	# at Constitution	Number in 1810	Founders	Pastors Prior to 1810	1810 Pastors	1810 Virginia Counties
Greenbrier	1781	12	-	-J. Alderson	J. Alderson	J. Alderson	Greenbrier
Big Levels	1796	14	58	-J. Alderson & J. Osburne	J. Osburne	J. Osburne	Greenbrier
Teay's Valley	1805	27	45	-J. Alderson & J. Lee	J. Lee	J. Lee	Kanawha
Mud River	1807	20	20	-J. Alderson & J. Lee	J. Lee	J. Lee	Kanawha
Kanawha	1796	12	33	-J. Alderson & J. Johnston	None	None	Kanawha
Cole River	1807	45	35	-J. Alderson & J. Johnston	J. Lee	J. Lee	Kanawha
Peter's Creek	1803	32	25	-J. Osburne & E. Hughes	E. Hughes	E. Hughes	Kanawha
Indian Creek	1792	23	61	-J. Alderson	M. Lacy & J. Alderson	J. Ellison	Monroe
Blue Stone	1804	12	-	-J. Alderson & Mr. Stanley	Mr. Stanley	None	Giles

In 1812 the Teay's Valley Association was formed and drew away a few churches, including Kanawha, from the Greenbrier. The Kanawha Valley Association was created in 1871, which Kanawha joined.

--source: History of the Baptists in Virginia by Robert Baylor Semple, published 1810.

Church organized 6th July <u>1796</u>

the Kanawha Baptist Church was organized by Elder James
Johnstone 6th July 1796
Nancy Morris offered and was received for Baptism May 27th
1797 wife of Benjamin Morris.
after preaching and prayer a motion by brother James
Johnstone to onvite the members of the different Churches to
a Seat in this association as messengers from them, and they
took there seat as <u>follows Bro Alderson and Bro Scags</u>
David Jarrett offered and was received. ~~Lucy~~ Susey [*Lusey*]
Jarrett offered and was received May 1797
    July 15/1797 it is ordered ~~that~~ by Brother Hud~~dlestone~~
Hudleen [*Hualeen*] and Seconded by the Church that Sister
Hud~~dlestone~~ be dealt with for nonperformance of her duties.
it is orderd that brother Hansford and Bro Jones to cite the
said Sister the next Church meeting
[?] Sister Hudleen Cited to the Church meeting and was
excused by reason of her not being able to attend

Brother Johnstone and brother Hansford promised to write
letters to the association and to the Society meeting and
[bring] them in next Church meeting
a Dore opened for Experience and Catherine Morris offered
and was received. William Morris received by letter and
experience
Sept 16th 1797   Adjuourned
Sister huling recd by Letter_____ _____

After praise and prayer, proceeded to business. 1st ~~Sister~~ the
letter to the Society meeting District and association brought
in and aproved of we Nominate brother Johnstone to bare our
letters to the District Society meeting and association October
10-1797
      Adjourned
Met according to appointment. after prayer proceeded to
business 1St Brother Johnstone Returned Brought in the

Letters and minutes from the District Society meeting and association and was read   Ajurnd

December 16th 1797

After prayer proceed to bussiness brother Thomas Trigg Recd by Letter

2nd sister Elizabeth Hansford whom Rcd as a trangent member to Communion ed returned to the Church from where she came

Ajurnd

Met according to appointment

Jany 2nd 1798

after prayer proceed to business 1st Brother Johnstone and Brother More appointed. to deal with Serting Members for neglect of attending to Church business

Feb 10th 1798

the Church of Kanawha met at Peters Creek after prayer proceed to business a dore opened for Experience___

Matthew Young offered and was received

Milley Young offered and was received

Brother Johnstone & Jones appointed by the Church to deal with certing members for omitting their duty.

March 17th 1798 the Church being met togather at the meatin house after prayer proceed to business the members Cited to deal with Certain members reported that they had Rcd Satisfaction ordered that the Church meatin and communion is to be held at Peters Creek on the third Lords day in August 1798   (adjurnd)

April 14th 1798 met according to appointment after prayer proceed to business

Brother Hansford Nominated to prepare a letter to the Soceeaty meeting and bring the same next Church meeting for Examinati.

May 19th 1798 met according to Appointment Prayer & Preaching. Proceed to business

1st the Letter brought in and Signed

2 Nominate brother Jenkins Jones & Hansford to bare our letter to the Society Meating

Ordered that Church meating Shall be held at Brother John Morrises on the Saturday before the fourth Lords day in June.

4th Sister Mary Shrewsbury Rd by Examination
     Adjurd
   1798
The minutes from the Society meating brought in and Read
and aproved
     June 21 1798

June 23 1798 Met agreeable to appointment at brother John
Morrisses after Prayer proceed to business
1st ordered that Silence Shall not be taken for consent in
Church business
2nd Polly Burl Rd by Experience
3 whether Shall we appoint another Church meating or not at
this place Answered not at present but occasionly
<u>4 Sary Baker Rd by Experience   (Members 54)</u>

July 14th 1798 Met agreeable to appointment after prayer
Proceed to business
1st ordered that the Decoram shall be red at every m Church
meating
2nd ordered that brother Hansford provide a letter and bring
in the same to our next Society meating
3) Nominate Brother Johnstone   1
    " Brother John Hansford   2
    " Brother John Jones   3
    " Brother Abram Baker   4
    Brother David Jarrott   5
    Brother William Huddlestone 6
    Brother Benjamin Morriss   7
    Brother William Morriss   8
to Set in our next Society meating
     Adjond

   1798

Met agreeable to appointment after prayer proceed to business
1st Sister Foster Rd by Experience

met Agreeable to Appointment at Kanawha Church Pr
1st Sister Marthy McCoy R^{d} by Letter

2nd Brother Upton appeared and acknowledged his fault and was restored to his Seat

3rd We Nominate our Brethren James Johnstone William Morriss and Edward Hughes to bare our Letter to the Association

4th ordered that brother Johnstone prepare the letter and bring in at the next Society Meating

5th	Lot R^d by Experience	(58)
6 wrong	Sary Alderson by Experience	(59)
6	John Baly R^d by Experience	(60)
7	Pally Huddleston R^d by Experience	61
8	Judah Fuqua R^d by Letter	62

November 17th Canawha Church   met Agreeable to Appointment after prayer poceed to business

1st the Church recomended Brother Hughes to Exercise his tallent in going forward to hold meatings in his neighboring Bretherns houses.

A complaint being laid in against Brother Warrick. Brother Hansford appointed to Cite him to next Church meating
Adj

December 15th 1798

Met agreeable to appointment after prayer proceed to Business Brother Hansford haveing Cited brother Warrick he appeared to answer the Complaint of of Sister Dolly and Baly thay not being present the Church thought proper to lay him under Cenchur until Next Church meating

Adj   1798

Jany 19th 1799

Met agreeable to appointment after prayer proceed to Business Brother Warrick continued under Cencher

Feby 16th 1799 being met togather after prayer proceed to business

1st Brother Warrick Continued under Cencher

2nd Motion by Brother Jones that Some other Member shall be Chosen to fill his place as a Deacon. referred till next Church meating)

March 16th 1799 The Church being met together after Devine Service proceed to business

1 Brother Warrick Continued under Cencher

2 Concluded by the Church that Brother Jones continue to fill his Seat in the Church as <u>deacon</u>

April 20th 1799 The Church being met togather after Devine Service
1st, Brother Warrick Continued under Cencher
2 ordered that Communion be held at the meating house on the third Lords day in June
3 Sister Fuqua Dismissed by Letter
4) Brother Johnstone appointed to prepare a letter with Brother Hansford to the next Society and bring in for inspection
5th Brother Johnstone appointed to bare the Letter
6 ordered that the Church meating be held at Brother John Morrisses the Saturday before the third Lords day in May

[first three items of April 20 repeated]
April 20 1799 The Church being met togather after Devine Worship proceed to business
1 Brother Warrick continued under Cenchr
2 that communion be held at the meating hous the third Lords day in June
3 Sister Fuqua Dismissed by Letter

May 19th 1799
then after prayer proceed to Business
1st Brother Warrick restored to his Seat
2 A Complaint Lodged by Brother Hansford against Brother Hicks the Church thought proper to order Brother Wm Huddlestone and Brother Benjamin Moriss to Cite him to the next Church meating
May 25th Being met togather at Brother John Morriss after Divine Service proceed to Sit to hear Experience^s for the reception of members Sister Lucy and Racheal was R$\underline{cd}$ by Experience

Brother Huddlestone and Morriss delivered their report
Brother Hicks came before the Church and gave them much satisfaction
May 25th 1799 2 Members appointed to sit in society.
1st Bro James Johnstone

2   Edward Hughes
3   William Morriss
4   John Morriss
5   John Moore
6   John Jones
7   Benj Morriss
8   William Huddlestone
9   John Hansford

2   by Brother John Hansford
appointed to write a letter to the Society and bring in at the
Society meating the Church being met togather AJ
the first Lords day in July
July 1799 (Elizabeth Proctor Rd
by Experience
August 17th 1799 the Church being met togather according
to appointment
1st the Church meating being opened by praise and prayer
2   Sister Marthy McCoy applied for a letter of Dismission
3   3 Brother Johnstone appointed to rite the same in bhalf of
the Church
                Aj
Sept Brother Johnstone appointed to write letters in behalf of
the Church to the Society and also to the association and
Brother Johnstone and Levy Morriss Nominated to bare the
letters to the Different Meatings
_____Adj_____
November 16th 1799
Church meating being opened Brother Warrick Laid in a
Complaint against brother Jenkins Brother Benjamin Morris
and Levy appointed to Cite brother Jenkins to the next Church
meating
December 15th 1799_____Adj
The Church meating being opened by prayer proceed to
Business
the Brethren appointed to deal with the Brother Jenkins Come
on and reported that Brother Jenkins did not give Satisfaction.
Brethren appointed to deal with ~~with~~ brother Jenkins again
Brother Johnstone and Hansford as the Church thought fit to
lay him under Cenchure for the present

2nd ordered the Church Covenant be red by the Clerk at our next Church meating

Jan 18 1800
Met agreeable to appointment after the Church Covenant being read by the clerk.

Feby 15th 1800
Brother ^asked John Jones what is the duty of a Deacon We think it the duty of a Deacon to Serch into all the Sekelar affairs of the Church

2 Brother Lewis Jones Rd by Letter

3 Motioned by Brother Morriss and Jones that there ~~be~~ shall be two Arms appointed to this Church and there be a Deacon ordained for each one one of them at Peters Creek and the other at the mouth of Cole River refered to until the next Church meeting

            ~~1799~~ 1800
March None Church meating by Reason of high Water———

April 19 1800 The Church being met together after prayer proceed to business

Brother Benjamin Morris haveing Brother John Nugen reports that he refused to come to the Church therefore the Church thought proper to appoint brethren John Hansford and William Huddlestone to cite him to the next Church Meating
3rd Brother Jarrett reported that he ~~reported~~ visited some Delinquent brethren and they Seamed pliable
4th Sister Jenkins continued under Cencher
July 18th 1800 Church being met according to appointment after praise and prayer proceeded to business
1st Motion to appoint Arms and Deacons to these arms
Answer the arm at Peters Creek is appointed and Brother Edward Hughes appointed Deacon
2nd the Arm at the mouth of the Cole reported to the next Church Meeting

3rd Brother William Huddlestone reported that Brother
Nugen gave no Satisfaction. the Church being informed that
it was out of his power to attend thought fit to weight til next
Church meating and send Send brother John Jones to cite him
to the next Church meating
4th Sister Jenkins gave full satisfaction and was Received into
full fellowship
        Adj
Aug 16 1800 Church being met togather after prayer proceed
to business
1st An arm appointed at the mouth of Cole River and we
recommend Brother Jonathan Hilyard to be their leader and
that a Church meating be held there on the 25 of this Instant
for their further regulation.
2nd Brother John Jones gave report to the Church that Brother
John Nugen Seemed obstinate. the Church thought fit to lay
him under Cencher
& Brother Benjamin Morriss and & Lewis Jones appointed to
Cite him to the next Church meating.
3rd Brother James Johnstone appointed to write a letter to the
Society meating and we nominate Brothers to Sit in Society
    James Johnstone
    William Morriss
    Benjamin Morriss
    John Jones
    Lewis Jones
    Edward Hughes
    Thomas Hilmon and
    John Hansford
       (Adj
   1800
September met according to appointment after prayer
proceed
1st Brother John Nugen appeared before the Church and
gave Satisfaction and was restored to his Seat in the Church
2 A Dore opened for Experience Mistress Welch offered and
was received but for Some circumstance was not Baptised at
that time
3rd Brother Daniel Booth applied for a letter of Dismission
ordered that the Clerk furnish him with the Same

4 that the Clerk prepare a letter to the Association and Brother Jones Johnstone & Hansford be the bearers thereof to the place apointed

The Church being met togather at the mouth of Cole River after prayer proceed to business

1st three Letters handed in and Received as follows

2 Fuqua R^d by Letter

3 Howard R^d by Letter

4 See   R^d by letter

5 A Dore opened for Experience

6 Daniel Boothe R^d by Experience

7 Sister Polly Burl Laid under Cencher

November 15th 1800

The Church being met togather according to appointment after prayer proceed to business

1st in Consequence of the many Complaints of extortion we Concluded to fix the price of Corn that is to Say not to Exceed three shillings pr Bushel at any time. and any member braking this rule shall be Liable to the cencher of this Church Ajd

December the 20th 1800

the Church being met convened togather after prayer proceed

1st we have Concluded the price of Hemp and Flax Seed not to Exceed one Dollar pr Bushel.____

Jany 17th 1801_____

the Church met togather after prayer proceed to business

1st Motion that the minutes of this Church be fetched in and forward next Church meeting and read.

Feby 14th 1801_____Ajd_____

The Church being met togather after prayer proceed to business

1st the minutes of this Church that is to ^{Say} the register or Church Book brought forward and read

2 Brother John Hansford and his Wife Jane appointed to Deal with Sister Kelley for omision of of duty and make report to the Church

3 ordered that Brother Johnstone and Baker Deal with brother Woods for nonperformance of duty and make report to the Church   Ajd

March 14th 1801
The Church being met togather after prayer proceed
1st Brother Hansford gave report to the Church that Sister
Kelley Seemed Pliable and she came to the Church and Seemed
to desire a reconciliation with the Church when she came
from ~~forward~~ and in conSequence of which she Sends a letter
to that Church hoping to have Communion and fellowship
with them and begs them to forgive her and Send her a Letter
of dismmission._____
2nd)—Brother Benjamin and Levy Morriss appointed to Deal
with Brother John Nugen for omission of duty and make
report to the Church_____
3rd) ordered that Communion be held at our meeting house
the third Lords day in June _____(Ajd)_____
April 18th 1801 Church being met togather according to
appoint after prayer and Exortation proceeded to bussiness
1st--Brother Benjamin Morriss reported that brother John
Nugen refused to hear the Command of the Church therefore
they thought proper to lay him under cencher. and ordered
that Brother William Morriss John Jones and John Hansford
deal with him and Cite him to the next Church meeting
   Ajd
May 16th After prayer & praises to God for his mercies
proceed 1st the Brethren ordered to Deal with brother Nugen
and cite him to the next Church meeting made report that he
refused to hear the Church. the Church therefore thought
him ripe for Excommunication but for Certain Reasons
suspended that Centance until next Church meeting
(2nd) Complaint laid in by Brother John Hansford Brother
James Johnstone therefore the Church orders brother David
Jarrott and brother Thomas Triggs to deal with him and cite
him to the next Church meeting
June 20th 1801
   The Church being met togather after prayer and preaching
a Dore opened to Experiences
1st Barbara holdmond offred and was Received Rd   71
2 the Brethren ordered to Cite Brother Hicks to the next
Church meeting made report to the Church that he refused to
come therefore they thought him Ripe for Excommunication
but for Certain reasons suspended the Centence till next
Church meeting___ (Ajd_____

till tomorrow at eleven o'clock
June 21 the Church being met togather
July 5th Davy offered and was Received.   72
    Hanna Wetch Baptise ---
        (Ajd)
July 18th Church being met togather after prayer proceed
1st the Declaration of the Centence of Excommunication
against brother Richard Hicks suspended till next Church
meeting   72
Novr 15th   The Church being met togather at the time   73
Novemeber 15th   & place appointed after prayer and praise
proceed to business_____
1st Brother Richard Hicks Continued under Cencher
2 the minutes of the Association brought in and read
    then   (Ajd)
December 19th
The Church being met togather according to appoint.
Meeting opened by Singing and prayer
then Brother Richard Hicks came forward and gave
Satisfaction and was restored to his Seat
       then Ajd
Jany 16th Church being met togather opened meeting by
prayer Singing   then we nominate Brother James Johnstone
to cite Brother Richards Hicks to the next Church meating to
answer the Complaint of the Church then (Ajourned until
next Church meeting
Feburary 20 1802
The Church being met togather after Devine Service proceed
and Enter on business
1st Brother By Christion[s] of the Church Cited Bro Davis
Alderson to apear before the Church therefore Brother Davis
came forward and gave satisfaction
2nd Rd by Letter a black Sister Nancy   74
      (Ajd
March 1802 No Church meeting by reason of Rain and high
water
April 17th The Church being met togather at the place
appointed after prayer a Dore opened to Experience
    Dinnah offered and was Rd
Motion to call James Stroud & Wife to account for omission of
duty in not Joining the Church we Nominate Brother

Johnstone & Jarrott to inquire into the reason and make report
to the Church.
Motion that Brother Thomas Hilmon inquire into the reason of
brother John Moses omission of duty in ~~attending~~ neglecting
attending Church meeting and make report to the Church
Motion that the names of the members ~~of~~ in the Body of this
Church be in rold by the Clerk and called over every Church
Meeting and all delinquent Members taken notice of
according to a former act of this Church
May 15th
     The Church being met togather at the Meeting house after
prayer and praise to God Brother Jarrott gave Satisfactory
report to Church and the delinquent Brethren

Brethren apeared and gave Satisfaction (Ajd)
July 18th 1802 The Church being met at the meeting house
after a discourse delivered by Edwards Hughes the list of the
members names being called we entered into business._
lst A Dore opened for to hear Experience_____
     Nicholas Jones Rd_by Ex   75
     Patsy Jones Rd by Ex   76
we nominate Brother Benjamin Morriss to cite Brother John
Jenkins to the next Church Meeting.__After a deliberate
consultation of the Church they authorise Brother Brother
Edward Hughes to exercise his gift in speaking in public to
Exhort or preach when ever he is called or feels inclined
     Pegga See__ Rd._____   77
August 15th
The Church being met [_togaf_]her at the Meeting house
Church Meeting being opened by praise and prayer the role
being called we ~~called~~ Chose Brother Hilmon moderator for
the present Meeting by reason of Brother Johnstones abstance.
____ then proceeded to business
1st Brother Benjamin Morriss made report to the Church that
brother John Jenkins refused to Come forward or to answer
the Church therefore they thought fit to lay him under
Cencher, and ordered Certain Brethren to Cite him to the next
Church Meeting
2nd after due delibertain the Church thought fit to Grant
Brother Hilmon the Liberty of Exercising his gift of Exhortation

as far as God gives light and Liberty any where in the bounds
of the Church
3rd Ordered that Brother Hansford prepare a letter to the
Association and bring in next Church Meeting for Inspection
                    Ajd
September
  After prayer proceed to business.
1st was to take notices of brother John Jenkins he was Still
found obstinate in neglecting to hear the Church. therefore
they thought fit to Excommunicate him and accordingly past
the centence._____
2 A A Dore opened for Experience
     Rachel Huddlestun   Rd   78
     Patty   -- —   Rd   79
3rd It is the opinion of the Church that our beloved Brethren
Hansford. John & Lewis Jones has the liberty of Exercising
their gift in publick within the bounds of this Church
4 the Letter brought forward and Brethren appointed for our
Messengers James Johnstone Edward Hughes and Richard
Hicks and to bare our Letter to the association   Ajd
[*in the above margins:*] September   October 16th
[*in the margins next to Jany 15th 1803:*] there was a mistake
in turning the leaves of old Book was too fast by one leaf .J.
            Jany 15th 1803
the Church being met together at the meeting house after
prayer and prayer
1st Mary Malone and Susanah Malone presented us with two
Letters of Dismission from the Church of Christ on Keppen
Hardy County & were both Rd
2 the Church next took up a refference from last Church
Meeting respecting Brother Davis Alderson and as he did not
attend neither Brother John Hansford that was appointed by
the Church to cite him to the Business was laid over till untel
next Church Meeting
3 the Church next took up the Petition from Peters Creek
under their consideration and after mature deliberation
concluded to grant them a letter of dissmission and
constitution and leave it to God and themselves to Choose
their own Pasture
Brother Thomas Triggs is appointed to Stir up Some Brethren
near him to a Sense of thier duty in filling thirr Seats in the
house of God both for worship and business   Ajd

<u>1802</u>
October 16th after prayer proceed to Business
1st by request of Brother and Sister Strong and Sister Patsy
Jones the Church orders the Clerk to give them letters of
dismmission
Nancy Jones R<u>d</u> for Experience   80
2 A complaint laid in by Brother Thomas against Brother
Davis Alderson for his unbrotherly conduct. therefore the
Church fit to lay him under Cencher (Ajd)

November 20th The Church met at the meeting house after
prayer proceed
1st Brother Davis Alderson continued under Cencher the
minutes of the Association brought in by Br Johnstone and
<u>read</u>

Dec 18 1802 Church met togather according to appointment
after prayer and praise to god for his mercies we proceed to
Business
1st Brother Davis Alderson not appearing at Church thought
fit to Send Brethren to Cite him to the next Church meeting
2nd a letter handed in by Brother Hughes for admission in
order for Constitution on Peters Creek where the Arm of this
Church now resides. Ordered that it be Postponed until next
Church meeting on account of the fewness of our members
and the Weightiness of the Subject
3rd Motion by Brother James Johnston that brother Hughes
be Authorized ~~to Publish the~~ by this Church to publish the
Exclusion of Certain Members in the Arm of this Church at
Peters Creek on the present occasion and no further
                    Then Ajd
Jany 15 1803 the Church met according to appointment after
prayer and praise 1 Mary Malone and Susanah Malone
presented us with two letters of dismission from the Church of
Christ ^{on} Sheppen Hardy County & were both R^d_____
2 the Church next took up a reference from last Church
meeting respecting brother Davis Alderson and as he did not
attend neither Brother John Hansford that was apointed by the
Church to cite him ŧ the business was laid over till next
Church meeting

3 the Church next took up the petition from Peters Creek
under thier consideration and after Mature Deliberation
Concluded to grant them a letter of Dismission and
constitution and leave it to God and themselves to Chuse thier
own Pasture
Jany 15/1803 Brother Thomas Trigg is apointed to Stirr up
some Brethren near him to Sense of there Duty in filling there
Seats in the house of god both for worship and business

February 19th the Church being met at the meeting house
after praise & prayer 1 Brother Davis Alderson continued
under Cencher_____
2 Brother Thomas Trigg and Sister Mary & Susanah Malone
petitioned for letters of Dismission Elder James Johnston also
ordered that the Church furnish the Same
_____ Adj
Mch 19 The Church being met at the meeting house
1 Church meeting being opened by prayers and praise. then
proceeded to Chuse Brother Lewis Jones moderator
2 ordered that Brother Benjamin Morris inquire into the
neglect of Brother John Morses Duty in attending Church
meeting and make report to the Church
3 Brother John Jones ordered to Cite Brother Richard Hicks to
the next Church meeting to answer a Complaint laid ~~in~~ by
before the Church by Brother John Bailey and make Report___
Brother Davis Alderson ~~Excomm~~ Excommunicated. and from
the Remoteness of our Situation and being at this time
destitute of an ordained minister we authorise and Command
brother John Hansford to publish the Same on the Lords day
next Church Meeting
5 ordered that the Clerk furnish Brother Thomas Hilmon
with a letter of dismission
April 16th 1803
the Church being met at the meeting house Chose Brother
John Jones moderator. the list being cald Brother John Jones
made a Report to the Church that Brother Richard Hicks
Seamed to give him Some Satisfaction about Comeing to
Church Meeting but he did not apear therefore the Church
thought fit to Lay him under Cenchur and Send Brethren
Benjamin Morriss and Lewis Jones to try to bring him to a
Sense of his Duty_ Brother John Morse Come forward and

Confest in not attending Church meeting and gave an Excuse
and Satisfied the Church

A Letter handed in by Brother Hansford from Peters Creek
requesting a Letter of Dismmission in order for a Constitution.

with instruction^s how to proceed the Church granted it and
ordered the Clerk to prepare a letter for tomorrow inspection
and then to forward the Same to the Peters Creek Arm of this
Church

Motion By Brother Lewis Jones that we Contribute to the
necessity of our Brother Abraham Baker as he has latterly
sustained loss by axident of fire.

Motioned Seconded and the Clerk ordered to rite to him to let
him Know who to apply to and thier Sums amunt

C

John Jones	Ten Bushel corn	10
John Hansford	Five _____	5
Levy Moriss	five _____	5
David Jarrett	three _____	3
John See	two _____	2
Benjamin Morriss	three _____	3
Lewis Jones___	three	3
Nicholas Jones	two _____	2
William Huddleston		5
Ajd		38

May 15th 1803 the Church being met togather Church
meeting being opened by praise and prayer proceed to Call
the role then to Business Brother ~~Lewis Jones~~
Benjamin Morriss and Lewis Jones report that Richard Hicks
refused to Come to Church meeting therefore Continued
under Cencher till next Church Meeting Motion by Brother
Benjamin Moriss and Seconded by Brother John Hansford that
an act of this Church Concerning the price of Grain and Seed
shall be repealed the Church took it into Consideration and
after a due Consideration of the gross iffects and the ill effects
that attended it It was unanomously agreed on and
accordingly ordered to record then Ajd_____

July 16th Church meeting being opened by prayer after the
List being caled proceed to Business

1st Motioned that the list that had been caled every Church
meeting did not apear beneficial to the good of the Church
therefore they thought proper ~~therefore they~~ to lay it down

and not practice it any longer.   motion by Brother Hilmon
that ~~it~~ two members be Chose to Set in the Assciation
Seconded and agreed that Brother Hilmon & Hansford Be
apointed.
motion who Shall rite the association Letter answer Brother
Hilmon & Hansford
       then Ajd
August 20th the Church according to apointment and was
opened by Singing and prayer then proceed to Business
1st Brother Warrick Rd
      then Adj
1803
Sept The Church met and was opened by prayer then proceed
to business. After making the distant brethren a Seat Business
caled for none being found a dore was opened for Experience
none offered
October 15th the Church met according to apointment after
Singing & prayer proceed to business but none being found
    Ajd____
Nov 19th the Church met and opened by prayer
1st Motion by Brother Hansford that Church meeting be held
at his house. Seconded and was accordingly apointed.
Brother Warrick laid under Cencher and Brother John Jones
and & William Huddleston appointed to Cite him to the Next
Church meeting, also to call on sister Catherine Morriss as an
Evidence against him
Dec 17th the Church met at Brother Hansfords after
interducing by Prayer proceed to call for references Warrick
apeared but not giving the Church Satisfaction was continued
under Cencher Ordered that our next Church meeting be
held at Sister Catherine Morrisis
1804
Jany 13th The Church met at Sister Catherine Morriss
interduced by Prayer the business called for
Warrick continued under Cencher and Brother Hansford
apointed to let him know that without Satisfaction he would
be cut of Next Church meeting
                           Adj
February 18 The Church met according to apointment after
Singing and Prayer proceed to business 1st Brother Warrick
Restored_____ Adj

Mch 17th the Church met according to apointment after prayer No business found_____

motion by Brother Hansford that Communion be held at our meeting house in June at the usual time Seconded by majority of the hole house

May 19 No business found   Adj

Jun 16th Church met according to apointment opened after prayer then proceed to business. A grevious complaint against Brother Warrick and it was ordered by the Church that Warrick be Excommunicated Brother Hansford apointed to visit Sister See and try to Convince her of her that she was living out of her Duty by neglecting to Come to meeting

July 15th Most grevious complaint laid in by Lewis Jones against Brother Nicholas Jones and being fetched in in proper order the Church thought fit to Excommunicate him which was accordingly done   Ajd

August 16th the Church met after prayer Brother John Jones and Benjamin Morriss apointed messengers to bare our letters to the Association. Nicholas Jones Restored   Ajd

September 16th Church met after prayer 1st Brother John Jones brought in an account against the Church which apeared Just and was Settled at the Stipulated Sum of one and Six Pense Each male member.   Ajd

October 20th the Church met at Brother Hansfords and was opened by Prayer then Proceed to business Brother Lewis Jones apointed to Deal with Brother John See for neglect of duty   Ajd

November the Church agreeable to apointment after Prayer Brother Lewis Jones made report to the Church that Brother John See gave him Satisfaction then Brother John Hansford apointed to Deal with Sister Jane Hicks for living out of her Duty

1805

December 16th The Church met at Brother Hansford after
Prayer then proceed to Business 1st Brother Hansford
reported to the Church that Sister Jane Hicks confest her fault
and apeared penetent with promises to come to the Church
though did not apear therefore the Church thought fit to
apoint Brother John & Lewis Jones to Deal with her
2nd Brother John Hansford & John Jones Sent to Deal with
Sister Racheal Huddleston for allowing unbecoming practices
in her house.
Feby 16th the Church met according to apointment and after
Prayer Brother John & Lewis Jones reported to the Church that
Sister Hicks proved penetent and accordingly Came and gave
Satisfaction to the Church.___the case of Sister Racheal
refered Brother William Huddleston Sent to Patsy Huddleston
to Deal with her for misconduct in her house
Brother Benjamin Morriss and Lewis Jones apointed to Deal
with Sister Catherine Morriss for allowing Evil practices in
her house.   Ajd
Mch 16th Church met at Brother David Jarrotts After prayer
Brother William Huddleston reported that Sister Patsy gave
him Satisfactory Excuse therefore it was Excepted.
Brother Benjamin Morriss & Lewis Jones reported to the
Church that Sister Morris gave them Satisfaction in her
confession and promises to attend the next Church meeting
therefore it was refered   Ajd
April 20th 1805
The Church according to apointment after Pr
the Case of Sister Catherine Morriss taken up she apeared and
gave Satisfaction 2nd the case of Sister Racheal Huddleston
taken up and Continued and Brother John Jones apointed to
Deal with her   3rd Brother Hansford apointed to rite a Letter
to Brother John Moss Concerning his living out of his Duty
4th Brother Benjamin Morriss apointed to visit Brother
Thomas Hilmon for living out of Duty
May 17th The Church met at the meeting house after Singing
and prayer Sister Racheal Huddleston apeared and gave
Satisfaction___2nd Brother John Jones apointed to visit
Brother Baker for omission of Duty 3rd Sister Mary Carrel
and Sister ~~Susanah Sun~~ Susanna Jarrott ~~and~~ apointed to visit
Sister Shrozebury. refered till next meeting (Ajd___

July 18th The Church met and was opened by Singing and prayer Sister Shrozeburrys business refered ordered that the Clerk furnish Brother John Morriss and pegga his wife with Letters of Dismission

ordered that Brother John Hansford and his Wife Deal with John Moss and his wife for neglect of Duty ordered that Brother Benjamin Morriss John & Lewis Jones be our ~~association~~ Delegates to the association and bearer of our letter

ordered that Brother Hansford write our ~~and~~ associate and Deposit it into the hands of the Delegates_____Ajd_____

[Note by margins by Sept 17th:] This is the man who established and organised the thi[rd] Baptist Church near where Aldersin is now

Sept 17th 1805

After an able Sermond Delivered by Elder John Alderson the meeting was opened by Prayer the case of Brother of Brother Moss refered.   Sister Hansford and Sister Jarrott apointed to Deal with Sister Shrozeburry for omission of Duty.____(Sally___Rcd by letter [*The line after Sally could be a ditto mark for Shrozeburry as it falls directly under the previous Shrozeburry.*]   ordered there be a collection made next Church meeting to Defray the Expense of the association_____ the minutes of the association and the Circular Letter presented by Brother Hans^ford and received with pleasure. also Subscription for to raise money to print a piece on the Subject or ordinance of Baptism. (Worrick Restored

Ajd

1805 Oct 19th The Church met agreeable to apointment the first reference Concerning Sister Shrozeberry Laid over till next Church meeting

2nd The case of Brother John Moss laid over. 3rd Brother William Huddleston & wife apointed to visit Sister Hicks for her omission of Duty   Ajd

November not Met

December 15th The Church met at Brother John Hansfords and was opened in order by Singing & prayer

Then Proceeded to Business
1st the case of Sister Shrozeberry (Dismist
2 the case of Brother Moss laid over till next meeting 3rd the
case of Sister Hicks laid over till Next Church meeting
4th ordered that the Clerk furnish Sister Polly Smith with
Letter of Dismission
_____January not met

1806
February 15th the Church was met and opened meeting by
prayer
1st the case of Brother Moss laid over   .
2nd__ Brother Baker Dismist by Letter
March 15th Church met and opened by prayer.
and case of Brother John Moss laid over   Ajd

April 19th   The Church met opened in Due order
1st the case of Brother John Moss taken up and most
Deliberately Discust and then laid over as a reference till next
Church meeting
            Ajd
May 18th The Church met being opened in order the first
business was Brother Mosses case it laid over till next Church
meeting
June 7th the Early meeting being opened the Church Set in
order a black member (Dolly) by name was Excommunicate a
black member Nanney was Dismist by Letter
A dore opened for Experience then Ajd till tomorrow morning
Eleven Ock__

Drusy Moss Dismist by Letter
The Church met agreeable to apointment Set in order
July Not Met

August 16th Church met at Bro Hansfords Set in order Bro
Hansford appointed to rite the Letter to the Assciation and
bare the Same   then Ajd
Sept   not   met
17/October Church met at Bro Hansfords after being opened
in order proceed to business
1 the first was to the Church rite to brother Lee Pertissioning
him to attend our next Church meeting.

2nd Brother Hansford presented the minutes of the association with the Cirkulur Letter which was red and R^d with pleashure
3rd Ordered that our next Church meeting be held at Brother John Joneses

> Ajd

November the Church met Brother John Joneses after being opened in order Chose Brother Lewis Jones moderator
1 Brother & Sister Jones apointed to visit Sister Caty Morriss and Strive to ~~Show~~ Convince her of the Duty She Neglected in not attending Church Meeting

> Ajd

December 22 the Church met at Brother Hansfords and was opened by prayer then proceed to business
1 the case of Brother John Moss Brought forward laid over till next Church meeting
2 Brother & Sister Jones Neglected to visit Sister Caty Morriss and was Excused and ordered to Still Proceed and ~~make~~ Report to the Ch   Ajd

Jan 10th 1807 The Church met and Set in order Sister Caty Morriss apeared and was Excused and was apointed to visit Sister Hicks for Neglect of Duty and make report
February Feby 14th   Ajd
    the Church met and was opened in order the case of Sister Hicks first. the case of Sister Caty Morriss not attending the Church apointed Brother John Hansford to visit Sister Caty for Neglect of her Duty and make report to the Church then---
Ajd
March Not meeting by reason of high Water
April the Same

May 30th Church met and took up the case of Sister of Sister hicks and she not being present the Church Laid it over till next Church meeting and apointed Sister pegga Childress to make her acquainted with the Circumstances.
2
A letter from Big Levels Church Concerning Mary Kelleys which was ~~received~~ red and naturely ConSiderd Sister Kelley being present after an experience of repentance she was received into fellowship

> Ajd

June 20 The Church met and apointed Brother Lewis Jones moderator and proceeded to business the case of Sister Hicks taken up and laid over till Next church meeting

ordered that Brother Levy Morriss vist Brother John Jones and inquire into ~~his~~ the reason of his non attendance of Church meeting and make report to the Church   Ajd

July 18th the Church met after prayer proceed to business the case of Sister hicks taken up ordered that Brother John Jones & wife visit Sister Hicks on that action and make report to the Church
    Jane Seat received by Letter
Brother Lewis Jones apointed moderator in place of John Jones
    ordered that Brother J Hansford prepare a Letter for the association to be red ⁱⁿ ~~at~~ next Church meeting for inspection

ordered that Br J Hansford J Jones Benj Morriss & Lewis Jones bare ~~our~~ ^{the} Letter to the Association and Set with the body there for business
       Ajd
To the Assn in 1807_____ 33 in Number

August 15+ After prayer the Church proceeded to business. the case of Sister Jane Hicks taken up she apeared in Church and was excused and was restored to the Church again. ~~accord~~ing to apointment of last meeting the letter to the association which was red and aproved of   Ajd
Sepr 1808
the Church at the meeting house opened by prayer then proceed the reference of last meeting Worrick haveing not apeared the Church thought fit to Send Brother Hansford to Cite him to apear tomorrow to answer the Complaint of the Church

Sister Caty Morriss haveing omitted her Duty in filling her Seat the Church thought Proper to Send Sister Carroll to visit her on that action
Sister Patsey Jones Rec^d by Letter

Brother Lewis Jones & wife Dismist by Letter

1808
Met at the place apointed meeting being opened in order the
first business Call^d for Sister Carroll reported that Sister Caty
refused to come to the meeting Defered until next Church
meeting

Met March 18th 1809
meeting being opened in order the case of Sister Caty Morriss
Morriss taken up. Br_ J_Lee apointed to visit S~ Caty on
account of a complaint laid before the Church and that he
should Direct her to apear at the Next May Meeting to answer
the Complaint Br J Jones apointed moderator
                    Ajd
May 20th 1809
      An able Discourse Delivered by E J. Lee Sister Caty Morriss
apeared and took her Seat. then Proceeded to Chose Brethren
J Hansford & B Morriss our Mesengers to the Greenbryer
Asociation
ordered that Br Hansford prepare a letter for the Same   Ajd
June 18th
      After an able Discourse Delivered by E. John Alderson from
these words how Shall we that are Ded to Sin live any longer
therein._____

After business being call^d for and nothing found   Ajd

October the 15th 1809
After a able Discourse Delivered by E John Lee no business
found___   _____   ___Ajd
March nothing Done - 1810   Ajd

May 19th -- 1810 no business   Ajd

June 16th No business   Ajd

August 18th 1810
      Brother Hansford apointed to write a letter to the
Association also Hansford and B Morriss apointed the
Mesengers to bare the Same   Ajd

December 15th 1810 Preaching by E .J. Lee No Business
being found   Ajd

February 16th 1811 Preaching by E J. Lee
No Business found   Ajd
April 23 1811
  A Complaint made to the Church by Br John Jones
concerning a black man named Worrick
ordered that Bro John Jones visit Worrick and Inform him that
the Church Sends for him to answer the Complaint at the next
Church meeting and then_____ Ajd

the Church met according to appointment
the case of Worrick was taken up and after a full Investigation
of the case he was restored to his Seat again_____
the Church met Oct 19th 1811
& proceed to business - the case of Worrick was taken up
Discust in part and Laid over till our next Church meeting
            and Ajd

March 15th 1812
The Church met the case of Worrick was taken up and after
careful Examination of the Matter a decision was had as
follows to wit. ordered that Worrick be Excommunicated and that a Publick declaration thereof be made on
tomorrow after Sermond _____

_____

A complaint laid before the Church by Br William Huddleston
Concerning Caty Morriss which was taken up and Discust.

Then apointed Br W Huddleston his wife and Br Benjamin
Morriss to visit Sister Caty Morriss and Direct her to apear at
the next Church meeting to answer the complaint and that
they should make report to the next Church meeting

Ordered that Brother and Sister Huddleston visit Sister Pegga
See on account of neglect of Duty and make report at the next
Church Meeting   Ajd
    The Church met April 18th
the case of Caty Morriss taken up and after being Dully
Discust the following ~~Decision~~ was had Determined on
ordered that Caty Morriss be Excommunicated out of this

Church and the Proclamation be made on tomorrow after
Sermond
The case of Pegga See was taken up and Discust her Excuse
~~was~~ received and then
                    Ajd
Sept 15th 1812
Chrislanes Spangler R<u>d</u> into the Church by Baptism
~~xxx~~ Brethren appointed to attend the association J Hansford

B Morriss ordered that B Hansford Prepare a letter for S<u>d</u>
association and bring in tomorrow for Inspection and then
                    Ajd
November 14th 1812 & 1813/1815
the Church met and not any bussiness apeared
the Church then   (Ajd)

May 1814
    The Church met at Union meeting house and not any
business being brought before the Church they then   (Ajd)

May 20th 1815
The Church at Union meeting and not any business they then
<u>Ajd</u>
August
the Church met and apointed Brother Hansford to prepare a

letter to the Teays (Tez es ^his way^) valley association and S<u>d</u>
Hansford and Brother John Jones apointed to be our
Mesengers and bare the Letter to the aforesaid association
then   Ajd
The church met October 14th 1815
and apointed Elizabeth Proctor [Procton] to visit Sister Pegga
See and inquire into the reason of her neglect on not
attending Church meeting   then Ajd

April 20th 1816
    The Church met acording to apointment and after Devine
worship Proceeded to business the first was a memorial from
Thomas Gap Church in Cullpepper County Concerning Some
matters and things in Controvercy between one Mikel Yates of
that Church and John Jones of the Church of Kanawha
Concerning a Certin Negro boy named Jonithan ~T~ requesting
this Church to take the Subject under Consideration and

Determine the matter between them acording to the Justice of the case from the Testimony brought before them__ The Church Set and after the memorial was red and all the testimony Produced they unanemusly agreed that it was thier Duty to take up the Subject which accordingly was done and the case laid over le until our Next Church meeting
then Ajd
1816
June the Church met and after Devine Services the case of Mikel Yates & John John Jones was taken up and then laid over until next Church meeting   then Ajd

August the 21st The Church met at the time of our association at the Dwelling House of John Hansford and after Devine worship the business of Mikel Yates and John Jones was taken up and there being Twenty one ministers and Mesengers Present from the Several Churches to wit twelve and all being invited to take a Seat with us the Business was Laid before them. the Church then and John Jones agreed to and did apoint a Committee of thier own boddy to Settle and Determine the case which was accordingly done; to wit John Young John Deering and Joseph Thomas Chosen by John Jones & John See Paton Newman & David Harbour apointed by the Church and Antony Hampton appointed by both. and after Examining all the Evidence on both Sides gave the following Judgment__   __   ____
We your committee after haveing Examined all the Testimony in the above Cited case are of opinion that B^r John Jones ought to and must give up the above Jonithan to the Daughter of S$^{\underline{d}}$ Mikel Yates who intermarried with our Gabriel Jones son of S^d John Jones

|John Young
|John Deering
Signed by us --   /Joseph Thomas
\John Lee
| Paton Newman
--- then ajd_____|David Harbour
| Antony Hampton

March 15th 1817

the Church met after prayer & preaching the Church set in order no business being found the Church (Ajd)

1817
July 18th The Church met no business being found
              then Ajd
April 18th 1818
the Church met and Elder John Morriss being Present after Sermond and prayer then Proceeded to inquire if any business was to be brought before the Church and none being found
Church   Ajd

Jun 20th 1818
the Church met and after Sermond Delivered by John See then Proceeded to business
Question asked by Brother Benjamin Morriss is it Disorder for a member of our Church to attend any Partyes of Dancing Eating and Drinking although not being one of the Dancers. Answer that we do think is Disorder and advise all our Brethren and Sisters to withdraw themselves from all Such Company.
Motion made by Elder John Lee to apoint to atten members to attend the Association Next ordered that Benjamin Morriss and Levy Morriss be apointed to attend our next association and bare our letter then (Ajd)

September 19th 1818
   The Church met according to order Sister Patsey Huddleston Dismist by Letter   then Ajd

October 17th
the Church met according to apointment After Sermond Delivered by John Morriss then Proceeded to inquire if any business answerd in the Negative
              then Ajd
the Church met July 31 - 1819
Nothing Brought forward only Brothren Hansford J Jones & Benjamin Morriss apointed to attend the Next association
              Then Ajd
The Church met Sept 18th 1819

Sermond by Elder John Young then a dore was opened for to hear Experience and Robert .S. Larroson offered was received by Experience and was fourth Baptised   then Ajd
John Hansford Clerk

March 2, 1820
The Church met according to order and apointment and after Sermond preached by John Morriss
Nancy Hudnall was R<u>d</u> by Letter
April 13th 1822
the Church met and after Sermond preached by Bro John Morriss the Church set in order.
ordered that the Union meeting be held at Brother John Hansfords
then Ajd
November 29th 1823
the Church met at Br John Hansfords Sermond preached by Elder James Elleson then Chose him moderator and proceeded to business. Brother John Jones came forward before the Church and made an acknowledgement of his misconduct by Intoxication Desiring the forgiveness of the Church in that Case and be allowed continue as a member of this Church as formerly the Church being reconsiled to Br John Jones by his Confeshion he took his Seat as ~~ushual~~ ushal   then Ajd

Dec 21st 1820
The Church met at Brother John Jones & no Business being found they then Ajd
John Hansford
the Church met at B^r John Jones an after Sermond Delivered by Brother McAboy no business, the Church   Ajd
First monday in April 1824 J Hansford

The Church met a Br John Hansfords on Saturday the 8th of April 1824 Sermond preached by Br or Elder John Morriss the Church Set in order and then Chose Elder John Morriss to take the pastoral care of this Church which accordingly he Proceeded to take his seat as moderator
then William Kinner Joined this Church by Experience ordered

that our next Church meeting be held at Br John Hansfords on the fourth Saturday in June. Next   then Ajd

June 26 - 1824 The Church met a Br Hansfords Sermond preached by Br John Morriss. then Proceed to apoint Bro Kinner Bro John Jones to attend our next association and bare our Letter
then ordered that Bro William Kinner have the Liberty of Exercising his gift in Exortation when it may please the Lord to call him.
    Ordered
that our next Church meeting be held at the Dwelling House of Nelson Priddy on Saturday immediately before the fourth Lords day in July Next   then   Ajd

Met at ^{the} house of Nelson Priddy 24 July 1824 according to apointment after Devine Service notice was given that if any person Chose to join the Church by Experience and Baptism there was then as opportunity and Immediately come forward Mary Campbell and made Known her desire to become a member of our Church and Proceeded to tell her Experience which was Satisfactory to the Church and She was received into the Church and Immediately after her husband Robert Campbell came forward and was also received by Experience. and the next day being ^{the} Sabbath were both Baptised and received into full fellowship Jane Hicks who Produced a letter from the Baptist Church of the Dry Ridge of Kentucky was Received into this Church then adjourned until meeting in Course
            John Hansford Clk
Sept 25th 1824
    the Church met Br John Hansfords after Sermond preached by Elder John Morriss a Dore opened for Experience & George Richards offered and was received Br John Lewis Rd by Letter

the Church at Br John Hansfords May 1825 Sermon preached by E Wm Wood ordered that our next Church meeting be held at Mr Nelson Priddys in this county   then Ajd

the Church met at Mr Nelson Priddys according sermon preached by John Morriss then Ajd

the Church met at Bro Hansfords Sermon preached by Elder
W^m .A. Wood & ordered that John Hansford and John Jones is
apointed to attend our next association   then   Ajd

the Church met at Br John Hansford May 1825 Sermond
preached by Elder W^mWood ordered that our next Church
meeting be held at Nelson Priddys in this County
                    then Ajd
the Church met at Mr Nelson Priddyes acording to apointment
Sermond preached by John Morriss

The Church met at Bro John Hansfords Sermond preached by
Elder W^m .A. Wood.
            this was all copied on other side JMJ
November 12th
the Church met at Br John Hansfords
Sermon preached by Elder W^m .A. Wood ordered that Bro Levi
Morriss and Sister Jane Jenkins visit Br Edmond Meadows and
inquire into the reason of the neglect of his Duty and also to
Examine into his Conduct concerning his liveing in Known
outbreaking Sin and request to him to attend our next Church
meeting in order to give Satisfaction in these things and also
to show Cause why he has not attended Church meeting
according to his Duty and according to our rule and order and
that Br Levi Morriss report to our next Church meeting
Motion that E W^m A Wood take the Pastoral care of the
Church. E Wood being present Consented so to do and
accordingly he took charge of the Church and apointed to
attend our next Church meeting and also to attend our
Church once each month for one year then Ajd
                    John Hansford Clk

December 10th

The Church met at Br .J. Jones^s sermon preached by W^m .A.
Wood. Br Levi Morriss reported to the Church that he had
visited Br Meadows according to the order of the Church and
that Br Meadows Denied being guilty of any outbreaking Sins
as reported and promised to attend our next Church meeting.

a Dore then being opened to receive members and none
offering the Church then adjourned   John Hansford Clk

the Church met at Br Levi Morriss January 7th 1826
Sermond preached by .E. Wm A Wood and the refference
from the last Church meeting was again Laid over until next
Church meeting
          then Ajd

February 7th 1826

The Church met at Br Benjamin Morriss[s] the case of Br
Meadows Laid over till our next Church meeting then Ajd

March 11th 1826
The Church met at Br Hansfords Br Meadows being present
his case was laid over until our next Church meeting
          then Ajd
April the 8th 1826
The Church met at Br John Jones Br Meadows case was laid
over until next Church meeting
        no business   Ajd
May 13th the Church met at Br Levi Morriss after Sermon
preached by E W[m] .A. Wood the case of Br Meadows come on
him and Sister Jenkins being present and haveing reconciled
themselves to each other the Church ~~meeting~~ Investigated the
matter it was ordered that the case be Dismissed
        then Ajd
June the Church met Br Benj Morriss[s]
————no business then Ajd
July the Church met at Br. Hansfords
  no Business then   Ajd

1826

August the Church met at Br John Jones after Divine Service
Br Hansford was ordered to write a Letter to the Association
Brother Benjamin Morriss and John Jones with himself
apointed to bare the Same as our messengers

A complaint was laid in by Br Benjamin Morriss to the Church of the Disorder of Br Campbell ordered that Br Hansford and Benjamin Morriss wate on Br Campbell and direct him to attend our next Church meeting to answer the Complaint and that they report to the next Church meeting then Ajd

the Church met at Br Levi Morriss Second Sabbath in (October)
report made by Br Hansford concerning Br Campbell and the case being considered was laid over until next Church meeting
     then Ajd
The Church met at Br Benjamin Morriss Nov 1826 the case of Br. Campbell was laid over until next Church meeting the Church then   Ajd

December the 11th 1826
the Church met at Br John Hansfords and the case of Br campbell being attended to and Br Campbell not being present the Church thought proper to apoint Elder W$^{\underline{m}}$ .A. Wood to visit Br Campbell and Inform him that if he did not attend the next Church meeting that he would be excluded from the Church for contempt in not hearing or attending to the order of the Church
January 2   1827 Saturday
the Church at Br John Jones and after Dvine worship the case of Br Campbell come on and Br Campbell being present gave satisfaction to Church and was restored to his Seat. (then Ajd

Feby 2 Second Saturday the Church the Ch met at Br Levi Morriss and after devine worship ordered that our Church meeting be on the Saturday immideately before the first Lords day in each month then Ajd

April 1827
The Church met at Br Benjamin Morriss Divine Service no business Ajd

May the Church met at Br Hansfords no business
    the Church Ajd

June the Church met Br John Jones after Divine Service no business the Church   Ajd

July the Church met at Br Levi Morriss no business after Divine Service Ajd

August the first Sabbath the Church met at Br Benjamin Morriss after Devine Service ordered that Br Hansford Prepare a letter to the next association and that himself and Br Benjamin Morriss & John Jones be our messengers to bare the Same thereto. ordered that Br Hansford Insert the following resolution in our Letter to the association and that our Delegates thereto be instructed to use thier Influence to have the Same adopted. that is to Say that when any Church Arm of a Church or any number [member] of our Brethren desires to have any Brother ordained to preach the Gospel it shall be the duty of the Candidate to wishing so to be ordained to visit each each Church within the bounds of the Association in which he resides and preach to them that they may be better able to Judge whether they are qualified to preach the Gospel or not which shall be Complyed with before any ordination shall take place in any of our Churches
                    Ajd
Saturday &
first Sabbeth in November the Church met at Br Levi Morriss Sermon preached by Elder Wm A. Wood no business the Church was Dismist   Ajd
first Sabbath in December Church met at Br George Richards Sermond preached by Elder W^m .A. Wood.
            the Church then Ajd
1828
first Sabbeth in July Church met a Br Hansfords No business Nancy ~~Harrimon~~ Harriman offered and was received but for some Circumstances of not being prepared her Baptism was postponed one month to be at our next Church meeting
            then Ajd
first Sabbeth in August Margaret Morris Second Wife of Levi Morriss offered and was received.
            Polley Elleson offered and was received. ordered that Br Hansford prepare a letter to the association then Ajd

Sunday ^{sabbath} after preaching Richard Hicks was restored to
his full fellowship. ordered that Br. Hicks and wife be Dismist
by Letter

---

the ordinance of Baptism then was administ[ered] to Nancy
Harriman Margaret Morriss and Elizabeth Elleson and then
Dismist   & Ajd
Sept 1st first Sabbeth met at Br Levi Morriss No business after
Prayer & preyes
              then Ajd
May the 1st Sabbath   1829
No business after Preaching prayer & preyes
              Ajd
Church met at Br John Hansfords Preyes prayer and preaching
by Elder W<u>m</u> .A. Wood no business
              then Ajd
June the 1st Sabbath
Church met at Br John Jones Preaching & prayer by Elder
Wood the Church ordered that Br Geo Richards visit Brother
Meadows to Know the reason of his neglect in attending
Church meeting and make report to the Church then   Ajd

July 6th 1829
The Church met a Br Benjamin Morriss After Preaching and
prayer & C   Brother Meadows apeared and Stated the reason
of his neglecting Church meetings which gave the Church
reason to believe that the [--?--] differences had taken place
with Sister Jenkins and himself and that it was necesary to
have both before the Church—wherefore the Church gave Br
Meadows notice that Sister Jenkins would be at our next
Church meeting to answer Some of the Complaints he had
laid in against her where he might have an oportunity of
investigating the matters of complaint the Church then
apointed Br Levi Morriss to visit Sister Jenkins and Inform her
of this bussiness and request her attendance at our next
Church meeting which is to be held at Br Levi Morriss house
      met next day the Sabbeath a Dore opened to hear
Experiences and black woman came forward the Property of
Thomas Busters widow gave Satisfactory relations of the work
of God upon her Sole and was received but was not Baptised
at that time by reason of her not haveing a Letter from her

[*mistress*] [*half a line is missing*] for her Slave to be Baptised
and become a member of this Church   then Ajd
August 1st 1829
   the Church met at Br Levi Morriss after Sermon preached by
.E. Wood the Church Set in order and Br Meadows and Sister
Jenkins both being present the Church took up their subject
and after Some Discussion Br Meadows apeared obstinate
which Terminated in his Exclusion from the Church.
therefore he is no more a member of this Church. the Church
then ordered thier Clerk to prepare a Letter to the next
association and apointed John Jones and Nicholas Jones &
George Richards to bare the Same.   then   Ajd
   The Church met at Br John Hansfords
Sept 7th 1829
   After Sermon preached by Elder W<u>m</u> .A. Wood
   no business found they then Ajd

October 2 1829
The Church met at Br John Jones after Devine Sirvis no
bessiness being the
          Church Ajd
April the 5th 1830 the Church met at Br Levi Morriss no
business the Church then
          (Ajd
May 1st 1830 Saturday
The Church met at Br Hansfords ^{business} ordered
June 5th   that the Clerk give Sister Polly Ellison a Letter of
Dismission from the Church
          then Ajd.
July the first Sabbeth
the Church met at Br John Jones after Preaching by Elder W<u>m</u>
.A. Wood
ordered that Brethren John Jones Levi Morriss & John
Hansford be apointed our messengers to the next association
and that Br Hansford prepare a Letter of fellowship for that
purpose and Deliver the Same to the association
          then Ajd
August met at Br Levi Morriss after Preaching on the first
Sabbath no business being found the meeting was then Ajd

Sept first Sabbath Church met at Widow Morriss no business
being found then Ajd
October first Sabbeth
the Church met at Br Hansford Polly Windsor [*Windson*]
offered and was received and ordered that she be Baptised
tomorrow it being Sabbath
1831   then Ajd

1831

The Church met according to adjournment after Devine Servis
a Dore opened to hear Experience October the first Sabbath.

A Black man name Simon told his Experience who was
received and was Baptised the Same day Immediately after
Polly Windsor [*Windson*] then Ajd

The Church met at Br John Jones first Sabbath in June no
business the Church Ajd
     The Church met at Br Levi Morriss first Sabbath July
ordered that Br Hansford prepare a letter to our next
association and himself with Br John Jones is apointed our
Delegates to bare the Same and Set in that Boddy to do
business then Ajd

August first Sabbath the Church met at Sister Nancy Morriss
the Letter written by Br Hansford Produced and approved
          no business found then Ajd

The Church met at Br John Hansfords on Saturday Imediately
before the first Lords day in October and on the next day it
being Sabbath three members was received by by Baptism and
Experience. Dennis a black man Samuel a black man Nancy a
black woman the Church adjourned to Samuel Shrewsberys
the next day when then three more members received two by
Baptism and one by Letter

Samuel Shrewsbury (Sener) by Experience and Baptism
   Mary Connehay by Experiences and Baptism
and Lucy Slack by Letter
          then Ajd
The fourth Sabbath in August 1831 being the time of our
association.

Sealey Harvey was received into our Church by Experience & Baptism

Polly Harmon was received also

Ajd

The Church met a Br John Jones first Saturday in November. no business being found they adjourned until Monday at Samuel Shrewsburys after Sermond and prayer the Church met accordingly and Set in order Rolly Shrewsberry was received Mrs Reese was received Mrs Slack was received Joseph Kurton [*Kenton*] was received

Harry a black man was received

Lucy a black Woman was received

Cloe a black Woman was received

A black man belonging to M. M. Fuqua (re<u>c</u>d

A black Woman belonging to Joel Shrewsburry received

All of them by Experience and was Immediately Baptised

A ~~man~~ woman belonging to Joel Shrewsburry received by Experience who had been Baptised before but who had no opportinuty of obtaining a Letter from the Church where She came from

_____then Ajd

May first Sabbath Church at Br Hansfords after Sermond a Dore was opened to hear Experiences <u>Sarah</u> <u>Hansford</u> <u>told</u> her experience and was received and was Baptised_____

Lucindy a woman of Couler offered and was received & was baptised

Third Sunday in May the Church met at Br Samuel Shrewsburrys after preaching by Elder W<u>m</u> .A. Wood. the Church Set to hear Experience. Thornton a man of colour offered and was received

1831

Third Sabbath in May Abraham a man of couler offered and was Rcd

Joseph a man of colour offered and was R<u>d</u>

All being Baptised fourth with Elizabeth Hartless R<u>d</u> by Letter

Miles a man of couler offered and was Received

Also Rebeckah a woman of couler was Recd by Letter and was Baptised fourth with then Ajd

first Sabbath in June the Church met at the house of Felix ~~G.~~
Hansford afer Divine worship it was ordered that Dennis a
man of Couler be Excommunicated from the fellowship of this
Church and that Elder W$^{\underline{m}}$.A. Wood publish the same fourth
with

first Sabbath in July the Church met at Br John Jones Polly
Jones offered and was Baptised fourthwith Edny was received
~~and~~ by Experience and Baptism fourthwith

1831
first Sabbath in August The Church met Br Levi Morriss no
bussiness Done Ajd
the Church received Sister Jene Wilson by Letter the 6th day
of August 1832 Also one other Sister -name not now
rcolected_____
Sept Saturday before the first Sabbath
the Church meat at Capt John Harveys [*Hurveys*] no business
being found the Church   Ajd

October Saturday before the first Sabbath Church met at Br
Hansfords no business being found then Ajd
James a man of couler received and Baptised

November first Sabbath Church met at Felix Hansfords no
business then Ajd

Nover the Church met at Felix Hansfords Elder W$^{\underline{m}}$ .C. Ligon
being present the Church Set in order Felix Hansford was
received and was forthwith Baptised   then Ajd

   1833
May 4th the Church met at ~~Br~~ Hansfords meeting house
prayer and preaching by Elder W$^{\underline{m}}$ .C. Ligon the Church
Chose him thier moderator and proceeded to business Felix
Hansford was requested to Exercise his gift in Exortation and
prayer at any time he might deem it proper (ordered that the
Church hold Communion tomorrow it being Sabbath then
_____Set to hearExperiences_____
Mary Jones widow came forward and was received

Moriah Moore came forward and was received
John McConinhey came forward and was received
Easter a black Woman forward and was Rcd
Nancy Blankenship came forward and was Rcd
    then ajd until tomorrow
at 10 oclock
Met according to adjournment at after Divine Service. the
Church met in order John Hansford Jr was received and all
the above was Baptised forthwith. then apropriate Sirmond
Delivered by E $W^{\underline{m}}$.C. Ligon the ordinance of the Supper
administered then Ajd until tomorrow at 10 oclock

The Church met according to Ajournment after Divine
worship notice was given that the Church Set in order to hear
experiences
    Moriah Hansford came forward and was Rd and fourthwith
Baptised on 7th day of May 1833

May 18th 1833
 The Church met at Hansfords meeting house Set in. order
John Harriman came forward and was Rd_____
Lucy Harriman came forward and was Rd and both Baptised
fourthwith by Elder $W^{\underline{m}}$.C. Ligon then Ajd

The Church met at Hansford meeting house May 15th 1833
    Lucy Pryor widow was received Rd
    Nancy Chapman was received
    Elizabeth Moore was received and all was Baptised
fourthwith by Elder $W^{\underline{m}}$.C. Ligon   then (Ajd)

May 16th 1833
The Church Set in order Nelson a man of Couler was received
    John Harriman Jr was received.
    Shadrick Harriman was received and all Baptised
fourthwith
        then Ajd
July 6 The Church met
Set in order to hear Experiences after preaching by Elder $W^{\underline{m}}$
C Ligon he being Chosen our moderator previously took the
Char _____
1 Milly Sims came forward and by

48 _____

2 experience was received
2 Polly Hudnall Same
3 Elizabeth Richards Same
4 John Sims _____ Same
5 Littlebury Shrewsberry Same
6 Mac[a]gah Hualson [*Hudson*] Same
7 Everet Moore   Same
8 Lucy a woman of color Same
ordered that Br John Hansford Sr prepare a letter to the Teayes
Valley Association and that Felix .G. Hansford John Harriman
S<u>r</u> and himself be our mesengers to bare the Same.
    then ajourned to 10 oclock tomorrow

July 6 1833 the Church met after praise prayer and
preaching by Elder W<u>m</u> .C. Ligon a Dore opened for
<u>experiences</u>
7 May [in left margin] <u>Winston</u> <u>Shelton</u> came forward and
was Rd by Experience and _____was Baptised
Francis Moore came forward and was received by Experience
    and Baptised then
    adjourned until tomorrow at ·
    _____~~10~~ 11 o'clock _____
Church met according to adjournment July 8th
    Alvah Hansford Received by Experience and was
    fourthwith Baptised_____
        then Ajd
July 14th
    the Church met a B<u>r</u> Samuel Shreusburys after preaching
the Church Set in order by E W<u>m</u> C Ligon John Shreusbury
the Elder came forward and was R<u>d</u>   W<u>m</u> Shrewsbury came
    forward and was Rd   then Ajd
July 15th the Church set in order John McCoy Received
then Ajd

1833
August 16 the Church met at Hansford meeting house and set
in order
Nicholas a man of colour was received
Elizabeth McCoy was received
Harriet Hudnell was received
Barbary Richards was received

John Richards was received
Miles Manser [*Mauser*] was received
all of whom was Baptised fourthwith /
       then Ajd

August 17 1933 Church at Br Samuel Shrewsburys meeting
house after preaching by .E. Ligon the Church Set in order
Samuel Shrewsbury Jr was received
Isau a man of colour was received
Lucy a woman of colour " received
James a man of colour   "   "
and ordered to be Baptised tomorrow
          then Ajd
Met acording to adjournment the Church Set in order
Milton Hansford was received
Abraham a free man of colour was received and all Baptised
except Milton Hansford who Chose to be Baptised at home

17th of 1833 August
Harrison a man of clour was received by Letter
         then Ajd
Church at Hansford meeting house and set in order
Anderson Hudnell was Rd and him with Millon Hansford was
       fourthwith Baptised then Ajd

the present number in this Church is 92-- the number
reported to the Association August the 25 - 1833
Church _____
met at Hansford meeting house first Saturday in Sept 1833
after Devine Service the Church Set in order
1st Robert Milburn was Rd by Experience
2 Wythal .A. Wood ' Rd by Experience
3 Sallie Pryor Rd by Experience
4 Nancy Harriman Rd by Experience
5 Emily Rili [*Rite*] Rd by Experience
6 Moriah Moore Rd by Experience
7 ~~Mor~~ Sary Starke " by Experience
8 Laura Shreusbury Rd by Experience
9 Mary Parks Rd by Experience
10 Wm Grinsted Rd by Experience
11 Polly Brannon Rd by Experience

12 BenJamin Jones R<u>d</u> by Experience
13 Sary Jones R<u>d</u> by Experience
first Saturday in September 1833 which was all fourthwith
Baptised
        then Ajd
the Church met at Shrewsburry meeting house the 3rd
Sabbath in September and Set in <u>order to hear Experiences</u>
1 Lemon Homes [*Hornes*] a man of color was received by
Received by Experience
2 Retter Homes [*Hornes*] a woman of color
3 W<u>m</u> Slack was Rd by Experience
4 Wm Rili [*Rite*] Rd by Experience
5 Page Stanley Rd by Experience
6 Samuel Burke Rd by Experience
7 Nancy Burk R<u>d</u> by Experience
all of which was Baptised fourthwith
        then Ajd
Feb ^{last of something}
and was allowed to take his seat again a leaf torn
_____ from the old book some record <u>gone</u>

Feby first Sabbath the Church met a Hansford meeting house.
ordered that the Clerk in future be requesed to read the
record of the last meeting of the Church Immediately after the
opening of the first Conference thereafter then to be Signed by
the presiding moderator and Clerk   then Ajd

1834
the Church met at Br Samuel Shrewsburys Feb 9th 1834
Herbert .M. Ledbetter Rd by Letter
    John Hansford
        Felix .G. Hansford
first Saturday in March the Church at Hansford meeting
house Brother Felix .G. Hansford apointed moderator for the
present meeting and no business being found the Church
adjourned

March 9th
the Church met a Br Shrewsbery meeting house Elder W<u>m</u> .C.
<u>Ligon</u> (Preached).
    Easter a woman of color

was R<u>d</u> by Letter
also Lucrecy [*Luerecy*] .S. Hannah
also John Turner
    then Ajd

The Church met at Hansford meeting house April 5th a Letter produced from Zoah Church by Edward Hughes requesting a Committee from this Church to meet a Committee from that Church to Settle a question with regard to the restoration of Edward Hughes whereupon the Church apointed W$^{\underline{m}}$ .C. Ligon John Harriman Felix .G. Hansford John Hansford S^r and Benjamin Jones to meet the Committee from the Church of Zoah in conference at Gauley Bridge upon that Subject then
        Ajd

Apr 12 The Church meat Br Shrewsburrys meeting house and received Sister Hashbarger by Letter and on the 13th Rd Nickor Smith   then (Ajd)

The Church ^{met} at Hansford meeting house on Saturday immediately before the first Sabbath in May and Rd by Letter
   Hezikiah Chilton also by Letter
   Henriettia Chilton
    then Ajd

May 31 st The Church met at Hansford meeting House Felix Hansford Chose moderator in the absence of W$^{\underline{m}}$ C Ligon--
the Committee apointed to meet a Committee ^{of} Zoah Church made their report that the time had not in their opinion arrived that Edward Hughes should be restored to the Baptist Communion and fellowship he being once a member of the Baptist Church and was expelled from that Society_____

ordered that the Clerk furnish Brother Ledbetter with a Letter of Dismission when applied for (applyed) for as he expects to move away
Yonsebus [*Yousebrus, Youselrus*] Hutchenson R^d and Baptised
   on Tuesday 27-- May
Saturday July 6th
at Hansford meeting house the Church met._____
Margaret Martin was Rd by Experience
 Joseph <u>Martin</u> " <u>Rd by Experience</u>
Galletin Hansford was Rd by Experience

have^{ing} been Rd previous thereto, was all Baptised fourthwith then Ajd
August 2
the Church met at Hansford meeting house after Divine Service the Church Proceeded to the business of the day whereupon Br John Harriman ^{Sr} Complaind of the bad conduct of his Slave Nelson he being a member of this Church and the man being present his case was immediately Investigated. which resulted in the exclusion of Nelson from the fellowship of this Church   ['July 6th' *in the margins*]

the ~~Church~~ Clerk was ordered to prepare a letter to Send to the next association and apointed Brethren Wm Shrewsbury Benjamin Jones and John McConnihay to bare the Same as our mesengers to the Associotion
the Church then proceeded to apoint four Deacons in addition to too that had been previously and whereupon John
Harriman Sr Miles Manser [*Mauser*] Wm Shrewsbury Samuel Shrewsbury with Felix .G. Hansford and John Hansford who was previously apointed and the ordination of them all postponed until the fifth Sabbath in August 1834

---

the Church met at Br Samuel Shrewsburys the 3rd Sabbath in August 1834
A Woman of Colour Rd named Nicey
Sopha a Women of Colour Rd by Letter
Julia McCoy Rd by Experience
     Dulittle Rd by Experience
A Woman of colour Rd by Experience the property of John McConinhay
          Ajd

August 10th 1834 The Church met at Gauley Bridge.
Catherine Manser [*Mauser*]
Ann Morriss
~~Lenn~~ Leneath Miller
Nancy Montgomery and
____Dorcus Slack Rd by Experience & Baptism
Aug 12   Wm Masterson
Samuel Masterson
Elizabeth Masterson

Jemmie Daviss
Nathan Wood
M Parkhurst
Susy King Rd by Experience & Baptism

August 24th the Church met at Br Samuel Shreusburys
Julean McCoy
Mrs Dulittle
Melindy a Woman of colour Rd by Experience and Baptism
_____

August 31 Church met at Hansford meeting House Sophia
Hix Rachel Hix Samuel McCoy
Jacob Grass Rd and Baptised

1834 Sept 1st Cynthia Hudnell
   Francis Shelton
   Rd and Baptised
Sept 21 Church met at Shrewsbury meeting house.
Corneleus Slack Rd by baptism.
Susanah Story   "   by B
Womslad [*Momslad or Wornslad*] a man of colour by B
Wyatt a man of colour by B
Widen a man of colour by B
Joseph Starke a of Colour Rd & Baptised
Pheba a woman of colour Rd by Letter
_____

The Church met at Charles Venables on the fourth Sabbath of
Sept No B Ajd
_____

The Church met at Shrewsbury meeting house Oct 19th__
James a man of colour R^d by Letter__ Henry a man of colour
" [*Rd by*] Letter
Lot a woman of Colour by baptism
Cynthia a woman of Colour by Baptism
_____ Ajd_____
the Church met at Hansford meeting house first Saturday in
October 1834 ordered that So many of the members as Belong
to this Church as may think proper has the liberty of
Constituting an arm to this Church at Gauley Bridge Meeting
House and is hereby authorised to hold Church meetings Do
Business receive members and to report into this Church

writeing the ~~names~~ number of the members they receive
annually one month previously to the Teayes Valley
association. and further ordered that Br Miles Manser
[*Mauser*] Be requested and is hereby authorized to hold prayer
meetings Exhort the people to good works and the necesity of
religion & C Signed by order of the Church.
John Hansford Clk

___

October 6th 1835 Church met at Hansford meeting house
        no business Ajd
met at Shrewsbury meeting house Oct 1835
A Woman of Colour the property of Wm Wilcox Rd by
Baptism
met at the Same place Nov 16th and Rd Nancy a woman of
Colour & Baptised
Also Rd and baptised Cog [*Coy*] a man of colour also Ben a
man of Colour the property of W<u>m</u> R Cox

1835 first Saturday in ~~February~~ January the Church met at
Hansford meeting house no business found, Ajd

Jany 19 Fortune & Nancy the property of James Hewit_____
        Dismist by Letter
Church met at Hansford meeting house after Sermon
Delivered by E W<u>m</u> .C. Ligon Br John Jones Complained that
Br Winsted Shelton had ~~reported~~ refused to Settle accounts
with him in a fare and Brotherly manner therefore he desired
the Church to interceed so far as to cause a Settlement
whereupon the Church ordered that Br John Hansford S<u>r</u> F
.G. Hansford & W<u>m</u> Earle. Be apointed a Committee whose
duty it shall be ~~apoint~~ to call upon both parties to produce
thier accounts and Evidence before the committee who shall
immediately proceed to Settle them in Equity and Justice to
both parties and make a report of thier proceedings to the
next Church meeting

Ordered that Br F .G. Hansford & Br W<u>m</u> Earls wate upon Br
Thomas Hix and direct him to apear at our next Church
meerting to answer a report that is in Surculation Concerning
his being intoxicated by Drinking Ajd

___

Adderson Ellerson ~~Lucindy~~ Mary Ellerson Lucindy Ellerson
Joined the Church by Letter
   Ajd
Third Sabbath in April the Church met at Shrewsburys
meeting house
Sam Wyatt joined by Letter
Edmond Damason by Letter
Jesse Womack [*Wornack*] by Letter
Anthony a man of colour by Letter
Mary Ruffner by Experience & Baptism
Kezia a Woman of colour by Experience & Baptism

May 1835
The Church met at Hansford meeting house the Committee
apointed to examine the case of Br Jones and Br Shelton
informed the Church that they were ready to report upon that
Subject but Br shelton not being present the Church advised
that the report continue in their hands until next Church
conference and that they Cite Br shelton to apear then on that
day to make his defence if he had any against Br Jones_____

the Committee apointed to visit ^{Br} Thomas Hix made report
that they have seen Br Hix and that he made Satisfactory
Confession of his misconduct and States he would apear
before the Church at the next Seshion but not being present
his case was laid over until our next Seshion
Eveline Spurlock Rd by ^{Ex} & Baptism [*in margin pointing to
Eveline:*] Shad Harimans wife
Jane Hudnall Rd by E_ & Baptism

May 17th 1835 the Church net at Shrewsburys meeting
house
Rd by Experience & Baptism
 Eli Dickinson a free man of colour
also a Woman of color belonging to Mr. Wilcox als ~~w~~ Squire a
man of Color belonging to Mr McDonel Ajd

June Saturday immediately before the first Sabbath Church
met at Hansford meeting
 Thomas Hix apeared and gave satisfaction

the Committee appointed to Investigate the difference between Br John Jones and Winsted Shelton

February first Saturday Church met at Hansford meeting house. After prayer ordered that W^m .C. Ligon and Felix Hansford be apointed a Committee to Inquire into the truth of an advertisement Seen in the Kanawha Banner, A Publick Paper Setting fourth that John Jones held a bond upon Winston Shelton which the S^d John Jones had fraudulently obtained from the S^d Shelton which he did not intend to pay and make report at our next meeting

Feby 1835 ordered that Br John Hansford Senor be apointed visit Sister Lucy Pryor and inform her that the Church requested her attendance at our next meeting to show cause if any why she should not be excluded from the fellowship of this Church for her refractory conduct in not paying a Sum of money to Br John Harriman after Church had investigated the matter and informed her that from the Testimony she ought to pay it. Ajd

March first Saturday The Church met at Hansford meeting house after prayer the Committee apointed to investigate the matter concerning Winsted Shelton and John Jones made report in the words following. the Committee apointed ~~the~~ to investigate the conduct of Br John Jones relative to a certain promisory transaction, between himself and a Mr Winsted Shelton reports that the Bond advertisid by Shelton in the Kanawaa Banner as having been fraudulently obtained was according to Sheltons own acknowledgement executed for the hire of a Negro man at a moderate price the Services of which Negro man the said Shelton acknowledged he had during the Term for which he was hired. therefore resolved ~~that~~ unanamusly that Br Jones be Dismist from further Censure as haveing been Guilty of in this transaction Either dishonest or immoral
Resolved that it is du to Br Jones and to the Kanawha Church of which he is a member that a copy of this record be insered in the Kanawha Banner
John Hansford Sr Clerk of Kanawha Church

March 7th 1836

Resolved that the Lords supper be administered to the Kanawha Church four times a Year in May and August at Hansford ^{at} meeting house and in June and September at Shrewsbury meeting house.____Resolved that a Collection be taken in the Congregation at each communion to aid in Supplying the destitute in this association with the preached word

the Clerk reports that he had visited Sister Lucey Pryor but did not receive full satisfaction
March 7th 1836 in the answer^s in the matter between himself and Br John Harriman therefore the Church continued her case and ordered the Clerk and Br John Jones to visit her again and report ~~at~~ to the next Church meeting
     Ajd
April the first saturday 1836
the Church met at Hansford meeting house the Clerk reports that he had informed Lucy Pryor Concerning the order of the Church and requesting her attendance at this meeting by the authority of the Church and Sister Pryor failing to attend according to notice or transmit any Communication to the Church affords us evidence of a detirmenation to disrgard the past recommendations of this Boddy and a detirmanation to treat Contem~~ptably~~tuously the Authority of this Church therefore resolved that she be excluded from the fellowship of this Church
     Ajd

May first <u>1836</u> Church met at Hansford meeting house. After devine Service Brother Littlebury Shrewsbury informed the Church that evil reports have gone out concerning the conduct of Br Jacob Grass that he thought ought to be inquired into and investigated whereupon the Church appointed a Committee of three ~~to~~ John Harriman Wm Earle and Milton Starke whose duty it shall be to give Br Grass notice that they will attend to that business on any certain day apointed by them where & when he is requested to attend with the testimony he may deem necesary. and if the Committee after examining such witnesses as they may see fit and have a full investigation of the case and think that he ought to be reported to the Church they shall proceed so to do to the next Church meeting_____

__ordered that the Check furnish Brother Hezikiah Chilton with a letter of dismission Ajd

June 4th 1836 the Church met at Hansford meeting house the Committee apointed to investigate the conduct of Br Jacob Grass reported which report the Church received and the committee discharged whereupon the Church proceeded to investigate the case and after examining the testimony thought proper to exclude him from the fellowship of this Church therefore Jacob Grass is no more a member of this Church Ajd

July first Sabbath ~~the~~ Moriah a Woman of color Rd by Baptism Pr of .J. Jones

Church met at Hansford meeting house
Julia Huddleston R̲d̲ by Baptism
ordered that the Clerk prepare a letter to the association and Elder W̲ͫ C Ligon & Brother Milton Starke be the barer of Same

Sept First Saturday ordered that E W̲ͫ C Ligon and Brother W̲ͫ Grinstead visit Br John Jones and inform him that the Church wishes an explanation ~~concerning~~ ᵒᶠ the matter concerning the burning of an instrument of writing between him and his Son Benjamin

ordered that B̲ʳᵉⁿ Felix Hansford John Hansford and W̲ͫ Grinsted visit Sister Shelton and request her attention at our next Church meeting to answer an unfriendly report that's gone out concerning her Conduct and all report to the Church

Oct no business

Nov̲ᵉʳ no business

Dec̲ʳ same

1837 Jany Same

Feb^r the Church met ~~at~~ first Saturday at Hansford meeting House and the Committee apointed to visit as above made report then [--]ed visited the Br & Sister and Satisfaction was given then by both Br Jones & Sister Shelton. therefore they was discharged from any further Censhur by the Church

Jany 1838 The Church meet first Saturday according to order Br John Harriman ^{Sr} called to the Chair a motion was made to further the consideration between the Two Sisters Hudnall & Sister Hudson (Cynthia Hudnall Br Hudson & his Wife were given Letters of dismission
a motion was made that the Church come to the following resolution resolved that the Church request thier Deacons to use all Diligence to procure some funds to compensate Elder W^m C Ligon for his Services in preaching from May 1837 until November the Same Year and that they make return of what they have done to our Church on the first Saturday in March next then Ajd
                J. H. Clk
March first Sabbath the Church met and the Deacons not being prepared to make report according to the former resolution therefore the report was postponed until our next Seshion   then Ajd

1838 saturday before the first Sabbath in April
the resolution as above taken up and was Continued until our next Seshion ordered that the Clerk furnish Jane Wilson with a Letter of dismission. Ajd-

May first Saturday the Church failed to meet,

Aug first Sabbath the Church met and ordered that Br Felix .G. Hansford and Br John Harriman be our next messengers to the next association Ajd

Aug 26 The Church met and Mrs Meadows wife of John Meadows come forward and Joined the Church by Experience & Baptism and on the 28th Edna Manser Matilda Windsor and Reuben Proctor came forward and Joined the Church by Experience and Baptism.

Sept 2 The Church met in order
Joshua Chapman come forward & Joined the Church by
Experience & Baptism. Also Francis Susan Harriman.__ Also
Sarah Hansford Daughter of Felix .G. Hansford   Ajd

1838 Sept 14 Church met
Francis Roberts came forward and was Rd by Experience &
Baptism

October 1st Elizabeth Grinsted was Received into this Church
by Experience & Baptism
        then Ajd
Oct 6th The Church and after prayer.
no business the Church then Adjourned until tomorrow
Eleven oclock
7th met according to adjournment Wm Morris was received
by Experience and Baptism   then Ajd

February 3rd Feby 1839
    The Church met and a request from Gauley Bridge Church
was presented praying that the Kanawha Church should Send
help to that Church to Settle a difference between Br Manser
& Br Williams wherefore whereupon the Church apointed
Elder W^m .C. Ligon Wm Grinsted Geo Richards John Richards
& Milton Starke to attend to that business
        then Ajd

Feby Mch 1839 March first Saturday Church met after prayer
and preaching by E W^m .C. Ligon the Church Set in order
ordered that E W^m .C. Ligon, Felix .G. Hansford & Br John
Harriman S^r waite upon Joshua Chapman concerning some
unfavorable reports that has gone abroad of him not
conforming with the Character of a Christian
    Also ordered that E W^m .C. Ligon and John Harriman Sr to
attend the meeting of the Central Committee to meet at their
Church the third Saturday in May next and both Committies
report t to this Church
        then Ajd
April first Sabbath the Church met and after preaching Sister
Mary Sandridge Joined the Church by Letter

ordered that the Clerk furnish Br Shadrick Harriman and wife
Eveline with Letters of Dismission
                    then Ajd
May first Saturday in May
the Church met no business   then Ajd

First Saturday in June the Church met Jennetta Morris Joined
the Church by Experience and Baptism

1839 June first Saturday Betty a Woman of colour Joined by
Baptism & Experience
July fifth Saturday No business
        then Ajd
August first Saturday the Church met and after divine Service
Set in order David Milburn offered and was received

The clerk presented a letter from Reuben Proctor one of the
members of this Church wishing to be dismist from the
Church whereupon a committee consisting of Felix Hansford
and Wm Grinsted was apointed to waite on Br Proctor and
inform him that he could not be dismist from the Church in
that way and to advise him to reconsile himself to the Church
and its members or Suffer Excommunication ordered that
John Hansford S<u>r</u> and John Harriman be our messengers to the
next
        Association   Aj<u>d</u>

Saturday before the first Sabbath in Sept the Church met and
after ^{sermon} delivered by Elder Bradley it was resolved that
Reuben Proctor be excommunicated from this Church which
was accordingly done   then Ajd

Saturday immediately before the first Sabbath in November
the Church met and after preached by Elder W. C. Ligon no
business being found

Saturday immediately before the first Sabbath in April the
Church met Sermond preached by E W^m C Ligon
   No business the Church Ajd

May   the Church met no business Ajd

July no preaching_____
August first ~~Sabbath~~ saturday Church met and appointed E
W$^{\underline{m}}$ C Ligon Br Geo Richards & Br J Harriman to bare our
letter to the association ___then Ajd
first Sabbath in August Church Set in order
Richard Grinsted and Wife Francis Rcd by Letter
Catherine Hansford Rcd by Experience and Baptism ___Ajd___

first Sabbath in Sept Church met and after Sermon preached
by E. W^m .C. Ligon. then held a Conference for the Colored
People and no business being then Ajd
First Sabbath in October Church met Simon a man of color
was Rd by Letter

1841 First Sabbath in May the Church met
    No business then Ajd

The first Sabbath in July the Church met and ordered that
W^m .$^{\underline{H.}}$ Grinsted and George Richards attend our next
association.
    October first Sabbath the Church
    met No business then Ajd

first Saturday in Febuary 1842 Church met and ordered that
the Clerk give Nancy Chapman a Letter of Dismission
            Ajd
March the first Sabbath a Woman of color name Judah the
property of Widow Morris Rd by Experience and Baptism
first Saturday in May the Church met Sermon preached by
Elder Mitchel then Set in order Ann Dempsey Rd and
        Baptised 1842
An application made for a Letter of dismission by the wife
Rolin Hudnell which was defered until the next Session
            Ajd

First Saturday in July 1843 Church met ordered that the
Clerk prepare a letter to the next assn and that W$^{\underline{m}}$ .H.
Grinsted be the barer thereof
        the case of Mrs Hudnell Still postponed until ~~our~~ next
meeting

October the 6th The Church met Sermon delivered by .E.
Wythel Wood the Church Set in order Jane Proctor Rd and
Baptised

December 31st Sermon preached by Elder Maloy Rock who
was there and then received into our Church by Letter of
Recomendation
Febuary first Saturday Church met in order no Business being
found then   Ajd

March first Saturday 1843
Church set in order the Clerk ordered to furnish Sister Sarah
Starke with a Letter of dismission   order that Elder Rock, Br
John Harraman & Wᵐ Grinsted wate on Joshua Chapman and
cite him to appear before this Church to answer Charges
prefered   Adj
May first Saturday the Church met Sermond preached by
Elder Mitchel ordered that the Clerk Br & Sister Wm Write &
Wife Letters of dismission from this Church
              then Ajd
1843 first Saturday in June the Church no Business then Ajd
until tomorrow no business being found Ajd

fourth ~~Saturday~~ Sabbath in June Church met in order Elizabeth
Pryor was Received by Experience and Baptism
John ~~Th~~ Tompson Rd by Experience
      and Baptism Ajd
July 16th The Church met in order
Reuben Hudson Wᵐ McConnihay Ire McConinhay and Joshua
Harraman Joined the Church by Experience & Baptism also
Antony a man of Colour by Experience and Baptism
          John Hansford Clk
                    1843
August first Saturday the Church met ordered that the Clerk
Prepare a Letter to the association and that Elder Maloy Rock
and Felix ᴳ Hansford be the Barrers of the Same and that Br
John Harraman and Ire McConinhay be thier alternates
sabbath day
Melvina Jones Francis Jones Sary Pryor Rd by Experience and
Baptism

First Saturday in Sept   the Church met motion ^{1st} shall we
send delegates to the Greenbryer convention \ Thereupon it
was resolved that Felix .G. Hansford .E. Maloy Rock & Br John
Harraman be our delegates to the Same.

Selina Shelton Rd by Letter
Francis Hudnell Rd by Experience & Baptism
ordered that the Clerk furnish Elizabeth Seesor
[Leesor/Susor/Sector, etc.] with Letter of dismission

Saturday Immediately before the first Sabbath in October the
Church met and after prayer the Delegates na that were
appointed to attend the Greenbryer Convention being present
Elder Rock rose and gave very Satisfactory State of the meeting
which was Rd by thanks. Br Felix Hansford rose and gave a
Satisfactory excuse Br John Harraman done the Same

the case of Joshua Chapman was taken up being called and
after some remarks upon the Subject it was finally decided to
Exclude him from the fellowship of this Church and
accordingly was in November then Ajd

The first Saturday in November Church met in order George
Roberson was received by Experience and Baptism then Ajd

Saturday Immediately before the first Sabbath in December
the Church met in order
no business appeared adjourned
until tomorrow
Met according to adjournment
no business Ajd
January & Febuary no business Ajd

1844
April 1st Saturday Church met in order Leah McCoy was Rd
by Letter
next day Sabbath Harriott a woman of
colour received by Baptism & [----]tion
May 4th Church met in order   then Ajd
a Committee was then appointed to Correspond with the
general association and request help in the minsstry from that
Boddy of Felix .G. Hansford John P Harriman and John

Hansford Sr next day Sabbath the Church met according to adjournment

Benjamin a man of colour Rd by Experience and Baptism

James Johnson was received by Letter

Francis Clark Sr Rd by Letter

Francis Clark Jr Rd by Letter

Harriott a woman of colour Rd by Experience and Baptism
                    Ajd

Saturday Immediately before the first Sabbath Aug the Church met in order. Resolved that E M Rock be our delegat to the Western general Association and that Felix .G. Hansford or John P Harraman be his alternate and that the Treashuror give him five dollars to entitle him to a Seat.

Resolved that the Clerk prepare a letter to the Teays Valley Association and that our Brothrn Wm H Grinsted and George Richards be the bearers thereof

ordered that the Clerk furnish Sister Windsor with a Letter of dismmission

Saturday immediaty before the first Sabbath in October the Church met in order the delegates appointed to attend the made Satisfactory report no business found the Church Adjourned until tomorrow morning Eleven Oclock

1844 Oct   sabbath morning Church met after Sermond by Elder Rock proceed to Set in order

Nov 3rd   Minney a man of colour Rd by Experience & Baptism

Saturday Immidiately before the first Sabbath in December the Church met no business being found
                Adjourned

1845 Saturday immediately before the first Saturday in Jany the Church met
      no business   Ajd

April first Sabbath Church met
   Roxelena Alexander was Received by Experience & Baptism

May first Saturday Church met
      no business the Church Ajd

July Saturday immediately before the first sabbath in July

Church met ordered that the Clerk prepare a letter to the Teays Valley Association and that Alvah Hansford and Ire McConnihey bare the Same and that Elder Maloy Rock and W<u>m</u> McConnihay be their Alternates
      then (Ajd)

<u>1845</u>
August   first Saturday the Church met & C ordered that the Clerk furnish Sister Edna Kincaid with a Letter of Dismission, then <u>Ajd___</u>

Dismission of Members
John Woods by Letter 1st
Elizabeth Hansford to her native Church
Judath Fuqua by Letter
Sister McCoy by Letter
Daniel Booth by Letter
Davy a man of colour
Brother Joseph Upton and his Wife &
Polly Burl
Drusey Moss
Nanny a woman of colour
Thomas Hilmon
Abraham Baker

Jane Jenkins	dead
Polly Jones died Sep 15 / 1851	"
George Richards	dead
Margaret Morris	died Sep / 1855
Francis Jones	Dead
John John	Died Jany 7th 1838
Edna Manser [*Mauser*]	
Polly Branham	died Sep 1861
Julia Huddleston	Died 1889
William Morris	" 1802
Matilda Windsor	" dead
Catherine Hansford	"
Jennetta Morris	Dead
Cynthia Hudnal	
Samuel McCoy	Died Sep 1846
Elizabeth McCoy died at Buffalo Putman Co	Dead
Polly Jones	Dead

William .H. Grinsted excluded	died 1859
Elizabeth Grinsted	died 1861
F. G. Hansford	died Mch/67
Sarah Hansford Sr	died
Sarah Hansford Jr	
John Hansford Sr	died Oct 1850
Jane Hansford	died Aug 12th 1854
Alva Hansford	died in 1889
Gallatin Hansford	died Sept 2 1853
Milton Hansford	Died Mch 1870
John Hansford Jr	Died 1878
no church Monroe Hansford	died in July 1908

Publick collection was made for E Wᵐ .A. Wood, November
12th 1825 for his first visit to take the pastoral care of this
Church to the amount of 5~~7~2 cents which was paid in
hand to Elder Wood

	5-7-2
December for the Same	2-8-1 1/4
January for 7 the Same	4-00
February 12 1826 for the Same	3 87 1/2
March the 12th the Same	4~1 2 1/2
April 8th for the Same	4 00
May 13th for the Same as above	4 ~ ~
July 10 its meeting Same	8~ ~ ~

Baptist Church Decorum or Decepline
1 the Church meeting shall be opened by and
Closed by prayer
2 A moderator & Clerk shall be Chose by the
members present
3 Only one person Speak at a time

UNPUBLISHED

COUNTY COURT RECORDS

OF WEST VIRGINIA

UNPUBLISHED COUNTY COURT RECORDS
OF WEST VIRGINIA

Introduction

Our ancestor, Peter Peck, first purchased land in Mason County, West Virginia (then Kanawha County, Virginia) in 1801. He was born in Lancaster, Pennsylvania in 1755 to immigrant German parents. His parents moved in his youth to the Shenandoah Valley, where he lived for about 30 years. During that time he served in the Revolutionary War four separate times. At about 45 years of age, Peter moved his growing family to Mason County where he lived out his days, dying there about 1832. Peter's eleven children married in and around Mason County, and there are still some of his descendants in the area to this day.

Trying to gather information about Peter Peck's family in Mason County, West Virginia was difficult. The microfilmed records of the Church of Jesus Christ of Latter Day Saints (LDS or "Mormon" Church) were searched, but there were many gaps in the information available on microfilm. There was almost no information before 1850. In 1982, we decided to make a trip to the area to see what local records where available on site.

Courthouse records in Mason County, West Virginia: 1850 to present

Hoping to find a contact in Mason County before going on the trip, we obtained a local phone book, picked out a Peck family from about 20 listed, and called Hazel Peck, wife of Homer Peck. As in so many genealogical searches, "coincidence" and "luck" played a very favorable part in finding the records needed. Hazel just happened to be a distant relative and the only Peck in the area actively doing genealogical research. She knew a great deal about Peter Peck and his family and descendants. My wife and I drove to Mason County to visit Hazel, who graciously received us. We traded information with this kind woman, and she gave us the names of others in the area also searching out Pecks and related lines. One contact in particular proved to be most helpful--Mrs. Russell Calvert, of Cabin Creek, WV.

After leaving Hazel's, we stopped at the Mason County clerk's office to see if there were any records for the members of the Peck family for the period 1800 to 1850 that had not been microfilmed. The clerk in the office stated that there were no records available from that time period. There was a fire in the County Courthouse in the 1850's, and that clerk stated that many of the records for the earlier years had been destroyed at that time. This was disheartening news.

On the return trip home to the Washington DC area, we also stropped at the State Archive Office in Charleston, West Virginia, the state capitol. The clerks in the Archive Office also advised us that there were no records available, that many of the Mason County court records before the 1850's were destroyed by the previously mentioned fire. Coming up empty, we started for home.

On the way from Charleston, we stopped at a gasoline station to inquire about directions on how to get to Highway 64. Cabin Creek was mentioned in the directions, so we decided to try to visit Mrs. Russell Calvert (the woman mentioned by our Mason County contact, Hazel Peck). Stopping at a grocery store in Cabin Creek to look in the phone book for Mrs. Calvert, we could find neither her name nor the town of Cabin Creek listed, and were thus about to continue on our trip. At that moment a man walked up and asked whom we were looking for in the phone book. Upon hearing that we where looking for Mrs. Russell Calvert, he said that he knew her well, since he was a genealogist, also. He showed us Mrs. Russell Calvert listed as Ellen Calvert in a larger town that held the consolidated listings of Cabin Creek. We found that she lived only a couple of blocks from where we were--another piece of genealogy "luck."

County Courthouse records of Mason County, West Virginia: prior to 1850

Ellen Calvert happened to be home, and we had a very fruitful visit. We exchanged information then, and again during another visit to the area, and we also wrote letters back and forth over several years. She gave us copies of several Mason County Peck marriages conducted prior to 1850 that were not on the LDS microfilm. Ellen told us about finding information on the location of the missing Mason County records (prior to 1850)--the ones supposedly destroyed by fire. She furnished the following account of the experience:

Mason County Court Records
by Ellen Calvert, July 1984

Before the Mormons provided libraries with microfilm of county records, it was necessary to visit individual court houses to research this material. It was on such a visit to the Mason County, WV courthouse early in the 1940s that I learned of some little known records housed at the West Virginia University Library in Morgantown, WV. My ancestors settled in Mason County about 1800 and remained there for 100 years. However, I could not find marriage and other court records for any of my families for the period prior to 1830 and again during the 1850s and 60s. As I had done in other similar disappointing situations, I went to the local newspaper to advertise for descendants. The elderly gentleman in the newspaper office told me that my records just might be among those in the University Library. I asked him why they would be kept there instead of the Mason County Courthouse. His interesting explanation follows.

When he was nine years old there was a fire in the court house. His home was near enough that his mother could see objects that were afire being tossed from the court house windows to a bonfire on the lawn. She ran over to the fire to see what was being burned, and to her horror recognized the court record books. She ran home and got a rake, broom, her nine-year-old son, and a wheelbarrow. The two of them raked the books from the fire and beat the flames out with a broom, then carried them home in the wheelbarrow. He said he had never worked so hard as he did that night. His mother, a staunch DAR member, knew the value of the old books and vowed she would never return them to the court house. The next day she hired a truck and driver to take the records to the West Virginia University Library.

Several years later when I began a determined effort to complete the research on my Mason County Ancestors, I telephoned the curator of the library and requested copies of records on my family surnames. I received 162 pages! The curator at the library did not know how the library acquired these records, nor did the personnel at the court house know they were there--nor do the thousands of people, who have and will use these records, know the debt they owe this one woman and her nine-year-old son.

UNIVERSITY OF WEST VIRGINIA AT MORGANTOWN

I visited the West Virginia & Regional History Collection in Colson Hall at the University of West Virginia in Morgantown during the month of October 1991 in search of the lost fire records. The associate curator, Mr. Harold M. Forbes and his staff, were very helpful. However, they knew nothing about the records supposedly delivered to the Library after the fire in the Mason County Courthouse. They indicated that the records for Mason County are on microfilm, and arranged for the viewing of these records (100 rolls of microfilm). It was evident that these microfilm records were those made by the representative from the LDS Genealogical Society, John Van Weesep, who had spent considerable time (about four years) copying the records onto microfilm.

For several hours the staff attempted to find the records for Mason County given to the Library after the courthouse fire, to no avail. The staff also searched for the Mason County marriages prior to 1850 of which we had copies (some of which Ellen Calvert had given us, and some we had received from their Library in 1983 by written request). The marriages we had were not on the index of marriages contained on the microfilm rolls, and could not be located at all. Clearly, the records had existed somewhere in the Library in the past.

The "Loose Files" at UWV Library at Morgantown, WV

Since the marriages could not be located, I pulled out the letter the Library had sent to me in 1983 along with the marriage record copies. The letter indicated that the records are located in what is known as the "loose files." Fortunately, the Mason County loose files are indexed. The index is in a large card file (Mason County Court index card file). A card for the marriage bond of my ancestors--James Peck to Katherine Dashinger in 1827--was in this file, indicating the exact folder in which the original marriage bond was located (one of the records that had been furnished by mail from the Library in 1983). The assistant curator stated that many of these loose files had never been microfilmed. (At this time, it was thought that the Mason County loose files had not been microfilmed, although they had. The curator just did not know where to find them that day on the microfilm). There is no direct evidence that these pre-1850 records in the loose files are the ones sent to the library after the fire in the Mason County Courthouse, but I believe they are probably one and the same. There are also many records from the early 1850s in the loose files that are not included in the bound volumes currently housed in the Mason County Courthouse covering the same time period. These later records could have come from the bound volumes saved from the fire as indicated in the report by Ellen Calvert, while some volumes from the same period could have remained at the courthouse. Even without proof of where the records came from, these loose files were a great genealogical find.

Availability of Early County Records from UWV Library at Morgantown

In 1983 when I originally received copies of marriage bonds stored in the Mason County loose files, the Library had sufficient staff to locate records using the Mason County Court card index file, make copies, and mail them. That is no longer possible. The assistant curator advised me that the Library now does not have sufficient staff to offer the services that they once could in the past.

There are apparently thousands of early county records that are available at the Library but are not on microfilm. The staff, under the direction of Harold Forbes, recently reviewed many of the bound volumes of county court records that have never been microfilmed. They selected 3,000 volumes deemed to have genealogical value. They are now in the process of microfilming these volumes. Among these are 114 volumes of early records for Mason County, which are primarily records of land transactions. The microfilming of the Mason County bound volumes was being performed the day I visited the Library. See **Table** II or a list of these bound county records currently being filmed.

Other Early West Virginia County Records at UWV at Morgantown

In addition to Mason County, there are **loose file records** for many other counties on file at the West Virginia & Regional History Collection in Colson Hall at the University of West Virginia at Morgantown. Some of the records are indexed, as are Mason County records, but other county records have been placed in the collection without being organized or indexed.

On May 18-19, 1992, my family made a second visit to the Morgantown Library. A personal review was made of the loose county files by special permission of the Curator, John A. Cuthbert. The loose files are stored chronologically in boxes (five boxes to a three-foot shelf). The curator has said that access to these files is available to researchers, although many of the loose files are on microfilm. Table III presents the status of each county's records. The microfilming was done by the Church of Jesus Christ of Latter Day Saints (LDS) Genealogy Department and a copy is available at the University Library and at the LDS Family History Library in Salt Lake City, Utah, or through any of the church's branch libraries around the world.

TABLE II
Projected Schedule for Microfilming
West Virginia County Bound Court Records

County	# Volumes	filming dates
Ohio	18	April 1989
Monongalia	54	July 1989
Tyler	34	Dec 1989
Webster	52	March 1989
Preston	60	June 1990
Lewis	68	Sept 1990
Hampshire	105	March 1991
Mason	114	August 1991
Marshall	136	March 1992
Morgan	148	Dec 1992
Wetzel	208	Nov 1993
	1060 Volumes	

Table III
Status of microfilming of county court records
as of May 1992:
Loose files and indexes of the loose files

	Loose Files		Index Card File	
	# of	Micro-		Micro-
County	Boxes	filmed	Indexed	filmed
Braxton	82	YES	NO	NO
Booke	156	YES	YES	YES
Fayette	18	YES	YES	YES
Hampshire	145	YES	YES	YES
Harrison *	120+	NO	NO	NO
Jefferson	136	YES	NO	NO
Kanawha	541	YES	YES	YES
Lewis	175	YES	NO	NO
Mason	192	YES	YES	NO
Monongalia	341	YES	YES	YES
Monroe	197	YES	NO	NO
Morgan	51	YES	NO	NO
Ohio	556	YES	YES	YES
Pendleton	~	YES	(1/2 drawer)	YES
Summers	99	YES	NO	NO
Tucker	~	YES	(1/2 drawer)	YES
Tyler	72	YES	NO	NO
Webster	15	YES	NO	NO
Wood	322	YES	Partial	NO

* Recent acquisition.

As indicated in Table III, index files (by surname, chronological, and by subject) are available and have been microfilmed for most of the loose files of counties' records. However, a complete index for the Mason County court records and a nearly complete index for Wood County are available at the Morgantown Library but are not microfilmed. This index file for the Mason County records contains seventeen drawers filed by surname, eight chronological file drawers, and five subject file drawers. Two additional drawers for Mason County are by subject, but one-half of these cards are for the period starting 1879 and contain some death records (starting 1902) and some birth records (starting 1899).

The index file for Wood County contains six surname file drawers with only one drawer for the combined chronological and subject files, with two cardboard boxes of index cards not properly filed.

The large number of marriage bonds in the Mason County loose files indicate that many marriage licenses during the period 1801-1850 are missing from the county records maintained by the County Clerk (Tommy Haynes) in Point Pleasant, West Virginia. The location of these missing marriage records, as discussed in this report, is still a mystery.

We reviewed some of the boxes of records for Wood County and found many land records, marriage bonds, probate records, and other miscellaneous court records that were very vital to our research--information that was unavailable anywhere else. Similar records are there for many of the other West Virginia Counties. This is a source of early West Virginia records that has been virtually untapped because so few people have any knowledge of the existence of these records, including state and county officials. Hopefully, now researchers will know where to go and what to ask to see when they get there.

BIBLIOGRAPHY

History of the Baptists in Virginia, Robert Baylor Semple, originally published 1810, republished

Old Kanawha Baptist Church, One Hundred Sixtieth Anniversary, 1793-1953, Shirley Donnelly, D.D., 1953.

Old Kanawha Baptist Church Minutes, 1796-1845, copy supplied by Ellen Calvert, Cabin Creek, West Virginia.

Pratt's Bicentennial Book, Opal Norton and Patty Nugent, 1976.

The Baptists of Virginia, 1699-1926, Garnett Ryland

Bro - Brother
Sis - Sister

COX, William R 55
DAMASON, Edmond 56
DAVISS, Jemmie 54
DAVY, ---- 19
DEERING, John 35
DEMPSEY, Ann 63
DICKINSON, Eli 56
DULITTLE, ---- 53 Mrs 54
EARLS, William 55
EARLE, William 55 58
ELLERSON, Adderson 56
    Lucindy 56 Mary 56
ELLESON, Elizabeth 43 James
    37 Polley 42
ELLISON, Polly 44
FOSTER, Sis 11
FUQUA, ---- 17 Judah 12
    Judath 67 M M 46 Sis 13
GRASS, Bro 58 Jacob 54 58-
    59
GRINSTEAD, William 59
GRINSTED, Elizabeth 61 68
    Francis 63 Richard 63
    William 50 59 61-62 64
    William H 63 66 68
H, J 60
HAMPTON, Antony 35
HANNAH, Lucrecy S 52
    Luerecy S 52
HANSFORD, ---- 54 58 Alva
    68 Alvah 49 67 Bro 9-14
    17-18 21 24-32 34 36
    39-42 45-47 Catherine 63
    67 Elizabeth 10 67 F G 55
    68 Felix 47 52 57 59 62
    65 Felix G 47 49 51-53
    60-61 64-66 Gallatin 68
    Galletin 52 J 31-32 34 37
    Jane 17 68 John 1 14-18
    21-24 26-28 30 35 37-41
    43-45 51 53 55 59 64

HANSFORD (cont.)
    John Jr 48 68 John Sr 49
    52 55 57 62 65-66 68
    Milton 50 68 Monroe 68
    Moriah 48 Sarah 46 61
    Sarah Jr 68 Sarah Sr 68 Sis
    28
HANSFORDS, Bro 25
HARBOUR, David 35
HARIMAN, Shad 56
HARMON, Polly 46
HARRAMAN, John 64-65 John
    P 66 Joshua 64
HARRIMAN, Eveline 62
    Francis Susan 61 J 63 John
    48 52-53 57-58 60 62
    John Jr 48 John P 65 John
    Sr 49 53 61 Lucy 48 Nancy
    42-43 50 Shadrick 48 62
HARRIMON, Nancy 42
HARTLESS, Elizabeth 46
HARVEY, John 47 Sealey 46
HASHBARGER, Sis 52
HEWIT, James 55
HICKS, Bro 13 18 43 Jane 26-
    27 31 38 Richard 19 21
    23-24 43 Richards 19 Sis
    27-31
HILMON, Bro 20 25 Thomas
    16 20 23 27 67
HILYARD, Jonathan 16
HIX, Bro 56 Rachel 54 Sophia
    54 Thomas 55-56
HOMES, Lemon 51 Retter 51
HORNES, Lemon 51 Retter 51
HOWARD, ---- 17
HUALEEN, Bro 9
HUALSON, Macagah 49
    Macgah 49
HUDDLESTON, Julia 59 67
    Pally 12 Patsey 36 Patsy 27

HUDDLESTON (cont.)
Racheal 27 Sis 33 W 33
William 24-25 27-28 33
HUDDLESTONE, Bro 9 13 Sis
9 William 11 13-16
HUDDLESTUN, Rachel 21
HUDLEEN, Bro 9 Sis 9
HUDNAL, Cynthia 67
HUDNALL, Cynthia 60 Jane
56 Nancy 37 Polly 49 Sis
60
HUDNELL, Anderson 50
Cynthia 54 Francis 65
Harriet 49 Mrs 63 Rolin 63
HUDSON, Bro 60 Macagah 49
Macgah 49 Reuben 64 Sis
60
HUGHES, Bro 12 22 Edward
12 14 16 20-21 52
Edwards 20
HURVEY, John 47
HUTCHENSON, Yonsebus 52
Yousebrus 52 Youselrus 52
JARRETT, Bro 15 David 9 24
Lusey 9 Susey 9
JARROTT, Bro 19-20 David
11 18 27 Sis 28 Sun 27
Susanah 27 Susanna 27
JENKINS, Bro 10 14 Jane 39
67 John 20-21 Sis 15-16
40 43-44
JOHN, John 67
JOHNSON, James 66
JOHNSTON, James 22-23
JOHNSTONE, Bro 9-11 13-14
17 19-20 22 James 9 12-
13 16 18-19 21
JONES, Benjamin 51-53 59
Bro 9-13 15 17 30 56-57
60 Francis 64 67 Gabriel
35 J 32 36 39 59 John

JONES (cont.)
14-16 18 21 23-25 27-28
30-31 33-35 37-40 42-47
55 57-59 Lewis 16 21 23-
24 26-28 30-31 Mary 47
Melvina 64 Nancy 22
Nicholas 20 24 26 44 Patsy
20 22 31 Polly 47 67 Sary
51 Sis 30
KELLEY, Mary 30 Sis 17-18
30
KENTON, Joseph 46
KINCAID, Edna 67
KING, Susy 54
KINNER, Bro 38 William 37-
38
KURTON, Joseph 46
LARROSON, Robert S 37
LEDBETTER, Bro 52 Herbert M
51
LEE, Bro 29 E J 32 J 32-33
John 32 35-36
LEESOR, Elizabeth 65
LEVY, Bro 14
LEWIS, Bro 15 John 38
LIGON, Elder 50 W C 62
William C 47-49 51-52 55
57 59-63
MALONE, Mary 21-23
Susanah 21-23
MANSER, Bro 61 Catherine
53 Edna 60 67 Miles 50
53 55
MARTIN, Joseph 52 Margaret
52
MASTERSON, Elizabeth 53
Samuel 53 William 53
MAUSER, Catherine 53 Edna
67 Miles 50 53 55
MCABOY, Bro 37
MCCONIHAY, John 53

MCCONINHAY, Ire 64
MCCONINHEY, John 48
MCCONNIHAY, John 53
    William 64 67
MCCONNIHEY, Ire 67
MCCOY, Elizabeth 49 67 John
    49 Julean 54 Julia 53 Leah
    65 Marthy 11 14 Samuel
    54 67 Sis 67
MCDONEL, Mr 56
MEADOWS, Bro 39-40 43-44
    Edmond 39 John 60 Mrs
    60
MILBURN, David 62 Robert
    50
MILLER, Leneath 53 Lenn 53
MITCHEL, Elder 63-64
MONTGOMERY, Nancy 53
MOORE, Elizabeth 48 Francis
    49 John 14 Moriah 48 50
MORE, Bro 10
MORISS, Benjamin 13 24 Levy
    24
MORRIS, Benjamin 9 14-15
    23 Catherine 9 25
    Experience 9 Jennetta 62
    67 John 10 Margaret 42
    67 Nancy 9 Sis 27 Widow
    63 William 9 61 67
MORRISS, Ann 53 B 32
    Benjamin 11 14 16 18 20
    23-24 26-28 33 36 40-43
    Bro 13 15 32 34 Catherine
    25 27 Caty 30-33 John 11
    13-14 28 36-39 Levi 39-
    45 47 Levy 14 18 31 36
    Margaret 43 Nancy 45
    Widow 45 William 11-12
    14 16 18
MORSE, John 23
MORSES, John 23

MOSES, John 20
MOSS, Bro 28-29 Drusey 67
    Drusy 29 John 27-30
NEWMAN, Paton 35
NUGEN, Bro 16 18 John 15-
    16 18
PARKHURST, M 54
PARKS, Mary 50
PRIDDY, Nelson 38-39
PROCTON, Elizabeth 34
PROCTOR, Bro 62 Elizabeth
    14 34 Jane 64 Reuben 60
    62
PRYOR, Elizabeth 64 Lucey 58
    Lucy 48 57-58 Sallie 50
    Sary 64 Sis 58
REESE, Mrs 46
RICHARDS, Barbary 49
    Elizabeth 49 George 38
    42-44 61 63 66-67 John
    50 61
RILI, Emily 50 William 51
RITE, Emily 50 William 51
ROBERSON, George 65
ROBERTS, Francis 61
ROCK, Elder 64-66 M 66
    Maloy 64-65 67
RUFFNER, Mary 56
SANDRIDGE, Mary 61
SCAGS, Bro 9
SEAT, Jane 31
SECTOR, Elizabeth 65
SEE, ~~~~ 17 John 24 26 35-
    36 Pegga 33-34
SEESOR, Elizabeth 65
SHELTON, Bro 56 Francis 54
    Selina 65 Sis 59-60
    Winsted 55 57 Winston 49
SHREUSBURY, John 49 Laura
    50 Samuel 49 54
SHREWSBERRY, Littlebury 49

SHREWSBERRY (cont.)
Rolly 46
SHREWSBERY, Bro 51 Samuel
45
SHREWSBURRY, ---- 51 Bro
52 Joel 46 Samuel 46
SHREWSBURY, ---- 54 56
Littlebury 58 Mary 11
Samuel 46 50-51 53
Samuel Jr 50 William 49
53
SHROZEBERRY, Sis 28-29
SHROZEBURRY, Sally 28 Sis
28
SHROZEBURY, Sis 27
SIMS, John 49 Milly 48
SLACK, Corneleus 54 Dorcus
53 Lucy 45 Mrs 46
William 51
SLAVE, Nelson 53
SMITH, Nickor 52 Polly 29
SPANGLER, Chrislanes 34
SPURLOCK, Eveline 56
STANLEY, Page 51
STARKE, Joseph 54 Milton 58-
59 61 Mor 50 Sarah 64
Sary 50
STORY, Susanah 54
STRONG, Bro 22 Sis 22
STROUD, James 19
SUSOR, Elizabeth 65

THOMAS, Bro 22 Joseph 35
TOMPSON, John 64
TRIGG, Thomas 10 23
TRIGGS, Thomas 18
TURNER, John 52
UPTON, Bro 12 Joseph 67
VENABLE, Charles 54
WARRICK, Bro 12-14 25-26
WELCH, Mistress 16
WETCH, Hanna 19
WILCOX, Mr 56 William 55
WILLIAMS, Bro 61
WILSON, Jane 60 Jene 47
WINDSON, Polly 45
WINDSOR, Matilda 60 67
Polly 45 Sis 66
WOMACK, Jesse 56
WOOD, Elder 43-44 68
Nathan 54 William 38-39
William A 39-41 43-44
46-47 68 Wythal A 50
Wythel 64
WOODS, Bro 17 John 67
WORNACK, Jesse 56
WORRICK, ---- 28 31
WRIGHT, Shane 13
WYATT, Sam 56
YATES, Mikel 34-35
YOUNG, John 35 37 Matthew
10 Milley 10

Biographies if the Authors

Regina Peck Andrus has been involved in genealogical research since her father and co-author first stuck her in front of a microfilm reader when she was 12 years old.

She served on the board and as a librarian at the Dayton Ohio East Stake Family History Library for two-and-a-half years while living in the area. As an Air Force spouse, she has moved all over the country with her husband, thus has had the opportunity to do research in many different libraries. She is currently living in the library-rich Washington, DC area and working on a family history of her Peck ancestors and their descendants.

Dr. Eugene Lincoln Peck earned his PhD in Civil Engineering. He retired from the National Weather Service as director of the Hydrologic Research Laboratory. He currently is President of the Hydex Corporation, a private consulting corporation. As a genealogist for over 40 years, he has held various leadership positions connected with the Church of Jesus Christ of Latter Day Saints (LDS or Mormon) Family History Libraries, where he now serves as the Stake Family History Specialist. He teaches genealogy classes, and edited the publication, "Genealogy Class Outline for using a LDS History Center and other Washington, DC Resourcces."

* * * * * * *